EMERGING ISSUES IN INTERNATIONAL ENVIRONMENTAL LAW,POLICY & GOVERNANCE

The Evolution Of International Environmental Law, Sustainability, And Justice.

INNOCENT OYORI

For permissions requests, write to the publisher at the address below:

Innocent Oyori Nyang'au

innocentoyori@gmail.com

Library of Congress Cataloging-in-Publication

Data: Nyang'au, Innocent Oyori.

Emerging Issues in International Environmental Law, Policy & Governance/ Innocent Oyori Nyang'au.
Includes bibliographical references and index.

<u>DEDICATION</u>
My Daughter Golda Kwamboka
My Eternal Inspiration for A Greener Legacy.

"For We Are Strangers Before Them, And
Sojourners, As Were All Our Fathers.

1 CHRONICLES 29:15

TABLE OF CONTENTS:

CHAPTER 1: LEGAL DIMENSIONS OF ENVIRONMENTAL RESPONSIBILITY NAVIGATING THE INTERSECTION OF LAW AND THE ENVIRONMENT

CHAPTER 2: THE DEVELOPMENT OF INTERNATIONAL ENVIRONMENTAL LAW TRACING THE EVOLUTION OF INTERNATIONAL ENVIRONMENTAL LAW ACROSS NATIONAL FRONTIERS

CHAPTER 3: A GLIMPSE INTO THE PAST, PRESENT, AND FUTURE NAVIGATING THE PATH OF SUSTAINABLE DEVELOPMENT IN THE FACE OF CLIMATE CHANGE"

CHAPTER FOUR: EXPLORING THE INTERCONNECTED CHALLENGES OF ENVIRONMENTAL, SOCIAL, AND ECONOMIC JUSTICE IN THE PURSUIT OF GLOBAL EQUITY.

Preface:

In conceiving this manuscript, "Harmony in the Global Commons: The Evolution of International Environmental Law, Sustainability, and Justice," My impetus derives from the profound connection observed on the gravity and need to champion a greener legacy during my tenure as a legal practitioner and lecturer of law. The catalyst for this endeavor emanated from a genuine desire to document the intellectual discourses that transpired during the academic engagements with my students, particularly at Maasai Mara University located at the epicenter of The Great Mara Triangle—an ecological marvel and the cornerstone of Kenya's renowned Wildebeest migration.

The lamentable circumstances surrounding the destruction of the Mau forest and the vulnerable state of Kenya's indigenous communities in the wake of climate change have been instrumental in galvanizing my scholarly pursuits. This book, therefore, undertakes a meticulous reevaluation of international law, scrutinizing Kenya's alignment with the global community concerning the dynamic landscape of International Environmental Law.

The book explores the relationship between the environment and the law, underscoring the critical imperative for environmental conservation. It examines the topography of international law, revealing its role as a steadfast guardian of our environment and examining its evolution, notably its impact on sustainable development.

I have made an earnest endeavor to confront a pivotal theme – The concept of environmental justice. Specifically, delving into how legal frameworks can be transformative for marginalized communities, and how the intersectionality of environmental issues underscores the urgency of equitable solutions. The main theme of this book is an urgent call to action to seek a path towards harmony, where legal systems become catalysts for global environmental well-being, particularly championing the rights of impoverished communities and in this pursuit equitable justice, and a sustainable future for all.

Acknowledgments:

Gratitude flows abundantly to the individuals whose unwavering contributions have enriched the pages of "Harmony in the Global Commons: The Evolution of International Environmental Law, Sustainability, and Justice." To my esteemed colleagues, whose insights and scholarly exchanges have served as invaluable catalysts, your collaborative spirit has truly elevated this work. Heartfelt appreciation extends to the dedicated students at Maasai Mara University, whose curiosity and enthusiasm fueled the intellectual discourse that inspired this manuscript.

Special acknowledgment is due to the indigenous communities and environmental advocates whose stories and struggles illuminate these pages, reinforcing the urgency of our shared commitment to a sustainable and just future. My gratitude extends to the anonymous reviewers and experts in the field whose constructive feedback has played a pivotal role in refining the depth and scope of this work.

Finally, my family and friends, thank you for your unwavering support, understanding, and encouragement throughout this intellectual journey. This book is a testament to the collective efforts of a community committed to advancing our understanding of environmental law and global sustainability.

CHAPTER ONE.

LEGAL DIMENSIONS OF ENVIRONMENTAL RESPONSIBILITY: NAVIGATING THE INTERSECTION OF LAW AND THE ENVIRONMENT

1.01. The Nature and scope of the Environment

The environment is intimately interlinked with life and the remote survival of species. The environment is also an integral foundation of all aspects of life. It provides the habitat to the diversity among species as well as the varieties of biological matter and living organisms that exist across varying habitats such as land, water, and additional ecosystems. These include ecological complexes such as the diversity of intra-species, among species, and ecosystems.

The constituent genetic resources and organisms collectively constitute existing biological resources that form the subject of discussion in environmental resources.The term environment is of ancient origin and derives from an ancient French word '*environner*,' simply interpreted as 'to surround or to encircle. The multiplicity and complexity of the environment's structure thus makes it phenomenal to define in the simplest of words. The environment has been described to denote the intricate combinationof physical-chemical, and abiotic aspects such as climate, soil, and biotic factors such as living things that act upon an organism or an ecological community and ultimately determine its form and survival.[2]

The Oxford dictionary defines the environment as the natural world in which people, animals, and plants live.[3]

These definitions seek to illustrate the network and web of nature's constituent elements, which comprise both living and nonliving matter as well as artificial and natural features formed out of divine and human activity. Sadly, however the term 'Environment' is one that everyone seemingly understands but none can define.[4] In the context of our surroundings and a broader sense, the term refers to the entirety of the socio-cultural, natural, biotic, and abiotic factors and conditions that shape individual human life or in the community of others.[5]

[1] Convention on Biological Diversity (1992) Retrieved from [https://www.cbd.int/convention/ [2]Britannica Encyclopedia 2023 *Definition of the Term 'Environment'* Retrieved from https://www.britannica.com/dictionary/environment

[3]Oxford English Dictionary 2023 *Definition of the Term 'Environment'.* Retrieved from https://www.oed.com/?tl=true

[4] Ronald B. Mitchell, et al., The International Environmental Agreement Database Project (2010),availableonlineathttp://iea.uoregon.edu/page.php?query=static&file=definitions.html.

[5]French Dictionary 2023 Definition of the word Environner Retrieved from https://www.larousse.fr/dictionnaires/francais/environner/30158 Environner

1.02. THE TRANSBOUNDARY NATURE OF THE ENVIRONMENT.

If the boundary waters of the two countries are contaminated, those countries will need to cooperate, as neither one can manage the problem alone. If prevailing airflow carries heavy metals from one area to another, those in the polluted area are motivated to influence the policies of the countries in the offending jurisdiction.[6] States, therefore, have an international obligation in cooperating across territories through a collective spirit of global partnership to enhance, conserve, protect and restore the health and integrity of the Earth's ecosystem. As competing demands on the global commons are increasing, so does the protection of the environment and the pursuit of growth give rise to all sorts of conflicts.[7] The obligation toward preserving and containing the deterioration of the environment and the destruction of ecosystems is both an individual and collective obligation; as such, the environment is indivisible and shared.

The award of the arbitral tribunal in the Trail Smelter case is frequently cited to support the view that general principles of international law impose obligations on states to prevent transboundary air pollution.[8] One of the fundamental questions in understanding this concept pertains to whether a polluting state does have the sovereign right to do whatever it chooses within its territory, even when its actions cause damage to another state, or does the injured state have a right of territorial integrity, which limits the polluting state's right to use its territory as it pleases. The pollution, resource utilization, or environmental damage was done in one country now is routinely seen to have impacts in other countries as established in the Trail Smelter Case in areas outside any country's jurisdiction, and even globally. The realization that a doctrine of absolute sovereignty over the environment means a given nation could be a loser as easily as a winner has led states to cooperate in protecting the environment, and from this has emerged international environmental law.[9] This reality is discernible from the Trail smelter case where Fumes from the Trail Smelter in Canada blew south into Washington State, causing damage to American agricultural communities.[10] And the hunting of fur seals by Canadian vessels in the Bering Sea made it

[6]*Ibidem,* Page 9, Para5.

[7] Louka, E 2006 International Environmental Law: Fairness, Effectiveness, and World Order. Cambridge University Press.

[8] Trail Smelter Arbitration (United States v. Canada), 3 U.N.R.I.A.A. 1905 (1941), Trail Smelter case, 16 April 1938, 11 March 1941, 3 RIAA 1907 (1941); R. M. Bratspies and R. A. Miller (eds.), Transboundary Harm in International Law: Lessons from the Trail Smelter Arbitration (2006).

[9] Ved P. Nanda George, (Rock) Pring International Environmental Law and Policy for the 21st Century 2nd Revised Edition.

[10] Trail Smelter case, 16 April 1938, 11 March 1941, 3 RIAA 1907 (1941)

impossible for the United States (which possessed the islands where the seals bred) to protect them against depletion and eventual extinction. In these and similar cases, the demarcation of states along territorial lines no longer sufficed as a strategy to avoid conflict.[11]International Environmental Law, therefore, does not seek to examine the physical composition and other elementary aspects of the environment but rather concerns itself with the law that regulates human conduct in his interaction with the environment, the legal principles necessary in the preservation of biodiversity, and environmental resources as well as in establishing the essential legal underpinnings of other critical socio-political aspects such as the sovereignty of states over natural resources, territoriality of the environment and the determination of control over matters incidental to the environment matters.

1.03. Natural resources, the Environment, and the Law.

Natural resources constitute a fundamental portion of the environment as well as a central subject of discussion in the field of international environmental law. Natural Resources refer to renewable resources, tangible and intangible such as soil, water, and non-renewable resources as well as Microorganisms, plants, and animals, including fish and forms of aquatic life, flora, and fauna. Natural resources exist in our natural environment in various forms, they form an integral subject of discussion when dissecting the infrastructure and regulations regarding various aspects of the environment including features such as the mountains, valleys, ridges, water surfaces, deserts, and other manifestations, in the natural environment, besides buildings and other structures borne out of human effort and skill that compose the artificial environment. The conglomeration of both subjects in the natural and artificial surroundings thus forms our collective *'environment'* the subject in relationship with the law. The integral subject of discussion entails legal issues that arise out of the utilization of environmental benefits and associated challenges. This is the basis for environmental policy as various environmental issues mirror deeply socio-economic and health implications of human life.

1.04. ENVIRONMENTAL BENEFITS AND ASSOCIATED CHALLENGES

a) Economic Benefits and Challenges.

The environment comprises the extraordinary aspects and combinations of support systems such as the Earth's location and positioning in the correct galaxy, the appropriate length, and distance from a star, the proper rotation that influences the change of season, the proper amount of

[11] United Nations, 2007"Report of the United Nation's Award between the United States and the United Kingdom relating to the rights of jurisdiction of United States in the Bering's sea and the preservation of fur seals." Retrieved from https://legal.un.org/riaa/cases/vol_XXVIII/263-276.pdf

protective stratospheric shield that prevents excessive, adequate temperature range, sufficient water resources sunshine, proper terrain, breathable air and atmosphere, energy and minerals, photosynthesis, the carbon cycle, the hydrologist cycle, living soils, flora, and fauna. The economic benefits of a healthy environment are significant and contribute to sustainable development and the overall well-being of societies. Clean air, water, and fertile soil support agriculture, ensuring food security and livelihoods for millions of people. Biodiversity provides resources for industries such as pharmaceuticals and biotechnology, fostering innovation and economic growth. Additionally, natural landscapes and ecosystems attract tourism, generating revenue and employment opportunities. Renewable energy sources, like wind and solar power, offer sustainable alternatives, reducing dependency on fossil fuels and mitigating climate change impacts. However, these economic benefits are accompanied by challenges such as environmental degradation, pollution, and climate change pose serious economic risks. The costs of environmental damage, healthcare expenses due to pollution-related illnesses, and loss of productivity can strain economies.

B)   The Exploitation Of Natural Resources, Pollution, And Environmental Degradation

The natural environment is a source of raw materials for industry. Environmental resources such as precious metals, crude oil, timber, and agricultural produce propel our infrastructure. The environment is therefore vital in the fulfillment of all other essential rights entrenched in law such as the right to adequate nutrition, right to clean water, the right of access to Medicare, recreation, as well as the enjoyment and expression of culture. The uncontrolled exploitation of natural resources however poses a danger to the environment through pollution and continued degradation of the natural environment through deforestation and depletion of water from rivers and swamps. Activities such as oil and gas exploration are extremely polluting activities that pollute the environment thereby destroying habitats and making the environment uninhabitable. The exploitation of natural resources, pollution, and environmental degradation present pressing challenges in the modern world. Unsustainable exploitation of natural resources, driven by economic demands, often leads to over-extraction, deforestation, and loss of biodiversity, disrupting delicate ecosystems. Pollution, whether from industrial emissions, plastic waste, or chemical runoff, contaminates air, water, and soil, jeopardizing human health, wildlife, and aquatic systems. Environmental degradation, including deforestation, desertification, and climate change, further exacerbates these issues, impacting communities, economies, and ecosystems globally.

These problems are interconnected, highlighting the urgent need for comprehensive, international efforts to promote sustainable resource management, reduce pollution, and mitigate environmental degradation.

c) Nutritional Benefits And Uncontrolled Exploitation Of Natural Resources.

The natural environment has continually provided humankind with a means of livelihood, food, fruit, flesh, and vegetable throughout the evolution of human civilization. The living environment's role in the health of individuals evolves as the world changes; increasing evidence suggests that human health is influenced by our way of living and dealing with the environment.[12]The environment plays an important role in the production and preservation of the genetic matter responsible for the human diet. Naturally occurring lakes, oceans, and seas are the source of Fish and seafood which makes up for the protein content of the majority of societies' diet. With current diets and production practices, feeding the world's populations is degrading terrestrial and aquatic ecosystems, depleting water resources, and driving climate change.[13] This calls for an urgent need to address the imminent danger of depletion of these resources through sound environmental practices that bolster sustainable consumption patterns. The nutritional benefits derived from natural resources are vast and essential for human health. Fisheries provide a significant source of protein, essential fatty acids, and micronutrients to millions of people globally. Forests offer wild edible plants, fruits, nuts, and mushrooms, enriching diets with essential vitamins and minerals. Agricultural ecosystems yield diverse crops, ensuring a stable food supply and a variety of nutrients necessary for balanced nutrition.

However, uncontrolled exploitation of these natural resources can lead to overfishing, deforestation, and soil degradation. Overfishing depletes fish stocks, impacting the livelihoods of communities reliant on fisheries and threatening the primary protein source for many. Deforestation diminishes the availability of wild edible plants and disrupts ecosystems, reducing dietary diversity. Soil degradation hampers agricultural productivity, jeopardizing food security. Sustainable management and conservation of natural resources are crucial to ensure a continuous supply of nutritious food, safeguarding both human health and the delicate balance of ecosystems.

---

[12]Maria Alzira Pimenta Dinis, "Environment and Human Health." Journal of Environment Pollution and Human Health, vol. 4, no. 2 (2016): 52-59. DOI: 10.12691/jephh-4-2-3

[13] Poore, J., and T. Nemecek. "Reducing Food's Environmental Impacts Through Producers and Consumers."27 April 2021.https://www.science.org/doi/10.1126/science. aaq0216#: ~:text =

d) Energy production, consumption, and sustainability issues.

Environmental resources are important energy sources. Some natural energy sources include coal, natural gas, biomass, crude oil, and hydroelectric power. Solar Energy provides the energy required for the production of food whilst water resources are utilized to irrigate farms and facilitate the cultivation of plant and animal matter bore out of the whilst sufficient energy is responsible for economic growth and development the exploitation and consumption of energy pose diverse environmental issues and challenges such as pollution and resource depletion for non- renewable sources such as coal and crude oil. It is hence critical to address energy sustainability issues for the sake of protecting the environment and preserving limited resources for the future generation. Energy production, consumption, and sustainability are interconnected aspects crucial for global economic development and environmental well-being. Energy production from fossil fuels, while meeting the world's energy demands, contributes significantly to greenhouse gas emissions, climate change, and air pollution. Transitioning to renewable energy sources such as solar, wind, and hydroelectric power is essential for mitigating these environmental impacts. Sustainable energy consumption involves improving energy efficiency, promoting energy conservation practices, and adopting cleaner technologies. Addressing sustainability issues in energy production and consumption requires international cooperation, policy reforms, and investments in research and development. Balancing the increasing energy needs of growing populations with environmental preservation is vital to ensuring a sustainable energy

future, reducing the carbon footprint, and fostering a more environmentally responsible global energy landscape.
Earth.

e) Modern communication, transport, and environmental degradation.

The environment is an important source of Biofuels, renewable energy, crude oil, and other raw materials that sustain transportation activity and infrastructure. The environment has shaped revolutionary forms of transport including water transport. The natural environment is responsible for the availability of hydropower, wind power, and animal power which are important aspects of transportation. Freight ships used in the haulage of cargo travel through lakes, oceans, and high seas to deliver the world's freight that includes industrial goods such as cars and agricultural inputs, and food across continents. These environmental resources are critical in communication and transport for international commerce and economic growth. Emissions from automobiles, ships, and airplanes are however known to contain heavy metal pollutants such as lead and other toxic gasses that deplete the ozone layer. Environmental regulations are especially important from this perspective in ensuring that transportation patterns promote clean energy use to reduce the carbon footprint as well as the effects of global warming. modern communication and transportation technologies have revolutionized the way societies function, enabling global connectivity and facilitating the movement of goods and people. However, these advancements have also contributed significantly to environmental degradation. The proliferation of electronic devices and data centers, vital for modern communication, leads to electronic waste and energy consumption, impacting ecosystems. Additionally, the transportation sector, reliant on fossil fuels, contributes to air pollution and greenhouse gas emissions, exacerbating climate change and harming public health. Urbanization driven by enhanced transportation networks often leads to deforestation, loss of biodiversity, and disruption of natural habitats.

1.05. Social Benefits and Associated Challenges.

a) The environment recreation, entertainment, and degradation.

The environment is an important resource as it pertains to recreation, features such as waterfalls, oceans, and mountains are recreation and entertainment. The environment in its abundance directly provides varied recreational utilities in various forms such as shades and beautiful sceneries. Others include Cool water springs, geysers, and geothermal springs that provide recreational and therapeutic platforms. These features also support novel sports such as mountain climbing, windsurfing, sand bathing, boat riding, hiking, swimming, deep-sea diving, paragliding, hot air ballooning, and beach games that have socio-economic imperatives on human life. There are varied concerns however about the pressure of pollution from recreational activities, especially as pertains to intentional and inadvertent pollution arising from diverse recreational activities. These environmental concerns necessitate vigilance in the preservation of such environmental resources to enhance sound conservation and utilization strategies to avoid degradation. Unchecked recreational activities can lead to environmental degradation. Pollution from tourism, such as littering and improper waste disposal, harms ecosystems and wildlife. Deforestation for tourist infrastructure disrupts habitats, while overfishing in popular tourist destinations depletes marine resources. Striking a balance between recreation and environmental preservation is essential. Implementing responsible tourism practices, promoting environmental education, and enforcing regulations can help mitigate the negative impact, ensuring that the environment continues to provide recreational enjoyment for future generations.

b) The exploitation of Medicinal resources and sustainable environmental conservation.

The environment is an important resource in the natural remedies drawn from herbs and other elements from the natural environment such as fungi and useful Bacteria in curative and therapeutic medicine for various ailments. Revolutionary plant-based cures such as penicillin have significantly contributed to the transformation of the science of human health. Penicillin which is a derivative of fungus is an important treatment for bacterial and fungal infections. Other ancient branches of medicine such as *Ayurveda, African traditional,* and *aboriginal medicine rely* upon natural remedies and concoctions made from plant bark, ground seeds, and dried leaves. These forms of knowledge allied to the natural environment are important in improving health standards and the quality of human life. The natural environment as a critical repository of curative and therapeutic resources should be conserved and protected to ensure these resources and traditional knowledge are passed on from generation to generation and utilized effectively through sustainable utilization patterns that are commercially beneficial to both societies, and human health and ecological conservation.

The exploitation of medicinal resources from nature is deeply intertwined with the concept of sustainable environmental conservation. Many medicinal plants and natural resources are essential components of traditional and modern medicine, providing treatments for various ailments and contributing significantly to the pharmaceutical industry. However, uncontrolled exploitation, such as over-harvesting or habitat destruction, can deplete these valuable resources and threaten biodiversity. Sustainable environmental conservation practices involve the responsible management of natural habitats, ensuring the preservation of medicinal plants and their ecosystems. This can be achieved through measures like regulated harvesting, reforestation efforts, and the protection of endangered species. Sustainable practices also include promoting traditional knowledge and indigenous practices that emphasize the sustainable use of medicinal resources. Conservation efforts preserve medicinal biodiversity and also support local communities, ensuring their access to healthcare resources and maintaining cultural traditions.

c) The role of the environment in the sustainable preservation of culture.

There is growing recognition that traditional knowledge and customary sustainable use underpin indigenous people and local communities' resilience to environmental change, including climate change, as well as contribute directly to biological and cultural diversity and global sustainable development.[14]The environment is an important resource that has shaped societal values and norms, the earliest civilizations of humankind and industrial lifestyles depended upon the environment for evolution, the Nile shaped the Egyptian civilization and contributed to the early industrial revolution. Environmental conservation is therefore an integral part of preserving culture; environmental regulations conversely, therefore, mitigate the risk of destruction of valuable tenets of tradition, history, and culture. The environment plays a crucial role in the sustainable preservation of culture by serving as the foundation upon which diverse cultural practices, traditions, and beliefs are built. Natural landscapes, ecosystems, and resources often hold immense cultural significance for indigenous communities and various ethnic groups. These environments provide the raw materials for traditional crafts, arts, and rituals, shaping unique cultural identities. Furthermore, the environment acts as a repository of traditional knowledge, ecological wisdom, and sustainable practices passed down through generations. Indigenous cultures, for instance, possess intricate knowledge about local flora and fauna, which is vital for their medicinal practices, agriculture, and food sources. Preserving the environment ensures the continuity of this knowledge, fostering cultural pride and identity. The earliest documented forms of art and civilizations are engravings on the walls of caves beside the most notable discovery of fire that has transformed cultures and endured the test of time. Other cultural indications of culture woven around the natural environment include art and painting styles evidenced by special dyes processed from plants and petal pigmentations.

In addition, environmental conservation supports eco-friendly lifestyles and sustainable practices inherent to many cultures. Traditional farming methods, water management systems, and eco-friendly construction techniques are often deeply rooted in cultural heritage and contribute to environmental sustainability.

---

[14]United Nations. "Foreword to 'Environment, Religion and Culture in the Context of the 2030 Agenda for Sustainable Development'." UNEP, 2016. [https://wedocs.unep.org/bitstream/handle/
20.500.11822/8696/-Environment,
_religion_and_culture_in_the_context_of_the2030_
agenda
_for _sustainable development-

d) The utility of the Environment on science archeology and anthropology.

Archeology and anthropology are important subjects that investigate the human past to establish the evolution of civilizations as well as the transformation of different aspects of human life. While Archaeology and other anthropological sciences form the basis of investigative proof that the natural environment has shaped our culture and ways of life, the environment provides the platform for studying associated aspects that remain preserved in time. Invasive and destructive human development and activity such as construction that involves deep excavation and deforestation threatens archeology's great reservoir in nature. These environmental resources must be protected as the environment remains the ultimate library of such significant knowledge that if destroyed may never be recovered. There is an urgent need for robust Environmental standards and regulations to protect and prohibit interference with sensitive archeological, cultural, and ecologically sensitive areas. The environment serves as a rich and invaluable resource for the fields of science, archaeology, and anthropology, playing a fundamental role in enhancing our understanding of the natural world, human history, and cultural diversity.

In the realm of science, the environment provides a wealth of data for ecological studies, climate research, and biodiversity analysis. Ecosystems offer valuable insights into species interactions, adaptation, and evolution, contributing to the advancement of biological and environmental sciences. Studying natural habitats also aids in understanding the impact of environmental changes, pollution, and climate fluctuations, essential for scientific research and conservation efforts. In archaeology, the environment acts as a repository of ancient artifacts, fossils, and historical evidence. Archaeologists explore natural landscapes to unearth clues about early human civilizations, ancient cultures, and extinct species. Environmental contexts, such as soil composition and geological features, help archaeologists determine the age and origin of artifacts, enabling the reconstruction of past human societies and their interactions with the environment.

1.06. NATURE OF INTERNATIONAL ENVIRONMENTAL LAW.

The law as defined is the discipline and profession concerned with the customs, practices, and rules of conduct of a community that is recognized as binding by the community and enforcement by a controlling authority.[15] Salmond describes the Law as the body of principles recognized and applied by the state in the administration of Justice.[16] The law is therefore used to denote a "legal order". It characterizes the regime of adjusting relations and ordering conduct by the systematic application of the force of organized political society or the whole body of legal Precepts that exists in a politically organized society.[17]Environmental law refers to a set of regulations and guidelines that regulate human conduct as pertains to all activities and interactions with the natural environment.

International environmental law is an extraordinary branch of law that's intricate to coherently organize into a whole. This is due to the lack of a global environmental organization such as the World Trade Organization (WTO), comprising streamlined dispute settlement procedures. In contrast, international environmental law comprises several loosely connected global environmental organizations, independent international environmental agreements as well as piecemeal governmental practices related to the use of the environment, united by an effort to promote international environmental protection and sustainable use of natural resources.[18]

1.07. Sources of International Environmental Law.

International environmental law covers matter incidental to aspects around biodiversity, climate change, ozone depletion, toxic and hazardous substances, desertification, marine resources, and the quality of air, land, and water. The sources of international environmental law include public international law sources as well as soft law that constitutes both binding and non-binding agreements.

1.International Conventions.

International conventions refer to written agreements between States. The agreements establish rights and obligations as pertains to a specific domain. The provisions of a convention must not contradict the *jus-cogens* or peremptory norms that bind all States.[19] Upon negotiation, drafting,

[15] Encyclopedia Britannica. "Internet." *Encyclopedia Britannica*, 8th ed., vol.9, 2009.

[16] Salmond, J. W. (1966). *Salmond on Jurisprudence*. London: Sweet & Maxwell.

[17] *Ibid*

[18] Timo Koivurova Basic issues in international environmental law Page 8

[19] Bouchet-Saulnier, Françoise. *The Practical Guide to Humanitarian Law*. Rowman & Littlefield

and signing of a treaty, States are required to ratify the treaty to become party to the treaty. Ratification represents the approval of the treaty by the Legislative organ of the party-state. Ratification involves the head of state, often with the authorization of the parliament. Treaties are binding only on States which become parties to them and the choice of whether or not to become a party to a treaty is entirely one for the State.

A resolution dealing with matters relating to the environment that adopts an international declaration is a non-binding instrument, but the principles contained in that declaration can play an important or even decisive, role in the conduct of States. This is especially evident from Principle 21 of the Declaration of the United Nations Conference on the Human Environment, on the obligation to refrain from causing damage to the environment of other States or of areas beyond the limits of national jurisdiction that have influenced the conduct of States to such an extent that the International Court of Justice has recognized the obligation expressed in the principle as part of the corpus of international environmental law.[20]

2.INTERNATIONAL CUSTOMARY LAW.

The relevance of custom as a source of international law has been debated. Some Scholars maintain that custom is an authoritative source of international law.[21] Customary law is the oldest source and the one which generates rules binding on all States. Customary law is not a written source of law. International customary law has two elements. First, there must be widespread and consistent State practice, Secondly, there must be *"opinio Juris"*, or "a belief in legal obligation; i.e. States must act in a specific manner because they believe in the existence of a legal duty to do so. The States concerned must feel that they are conforming to what amounts to a legal obligation."[22]

3.GENERAL PRINCIPLES OF LAW.

The Statute of the International Court of Justice stipulates that 'the general principles of law recognized by civilized nations' constitute one of the sources of international law to be applied by the Court. General principles of law are primarily significant in filling gaps where treaties or customary international law do not provide a rule of decision.[23] Public international law, as

Publishers, 1998.

[20]International Court of Justice. "Advisory Opinion regarding the Legality of the Threat or Utilization of Nuclear Armament." Para. 29. Advisory Opinion of 8 July 1996.

[21] Anthony D'Amato, The Concept of Custom in International Law (1971)

[22] The North Sea Continental Shelf cases, ICJ Reps, 1969, p. 3 at 44.

[23] *International Court of Justice Statute.* Article 38: "The Court, whose function is to decide in

classically conceived, recognizes the Statute of the International Court of Justice as laying out the authorized sources of international law. Article 38 of the Statue identifies, inter alia, international conventions, whether general or particular, as a source of international law that the Court must apply when deciding disputes submitted to it.[24] 'The general principles of law include general principles of fairness and justice which are applied universally in legal systems around the world. The general principles of law are critical in Environmental matters and the making of decisions at international courts and tribunals.

4.JUDICIAL DECISIONS.

Judicial precedent is the source of law where past decisions create law for Judges to refer back to for guidance in future cases. A precedent is a principle or rule established in a previous legal case that is either binding on or persuasive without going to courts for a court or other tribunal when deciding subsequent cases with similar issues or facts.

A judicial decision that is binding on other equal or lower courts in the same jurisdiction as to its conclusion on a point of law, and may also be persuasive to courts in other jurisdictions, in Subse quent cases involving sufficiently similar facts

1.08. WHETHER ENVIRONMENTAL LAW IS A DISTINCT BRANCH OF LAW?

In answering the question as to the existence of a distinct branch of law known as *"Environmental law"* it is pertinent to examine the underlying concepts that apply in the scope of environmental law. They include aspects in both Private International Law, Public International Law, Criminal Law, and The Law of Torts, among other areas of law, in a practical perspective for instance, whenever a person either through an act or omission concerning the environment affects the private rights of a citizen from which act civil liability arises, that person is considered to have committed a tort which may include nuisance or trespass. Although in the realm of environmental law under the subject matter, the applicable law is the law of tort whilst in another perspective where a person engages in a forbidden act or omission under the statute for instance killing a wild animal, without statutory authority constitutes an offense under criminal law.

accordance with international law such disputes as are submitted to it, shall apply: a. international conventions, whether general or particular, establishing rules expressly recognized by the contesting states; b. international custom, as evidence of a general practice accepted as law; c. the general principles of law recognized by civilized nations; d. subject to the provisions of Article 59, judicial decisions and the teachings of the most highly qualified publicists of the various nations, as subsidiary means for the determination of rules of law."

[24]Orellana, Marcos A. "Typology of Instruments of Public Environmental International Law." Digital repository Beta, Page 8, paragraph 4.

the statute. Environmental law does not, therefore, exist as a distinct branch of law but rather as a collective bundle of regulations and statutes that seek to protect and preserve the sanctity of the environment and the enjoyment of all associated rights.

1.09. WHAT IS THE SCOPE OF ENVIRONMENTAL LAW?

Environmental rule of law is fundamental in the attainment of sustainable development goals. Environmental law assimilates environmental needs with the essential elements of the rule of law, it is especially important in providing the basis for improving environmental governance, by connecting environmental sustainability with fundamental rights and obligations.[25] The subject of environmental law encompasses diverse aspects of law including basic and complex concepts that are found in both common laws as well as other branches of law.

International environmental law on the other hand faces a very rapidly changing world characterized by an escalating trend of political power applied outside conventional governmental structures, in global and regional international organizations, or multinational companies. International environmental governance attempts to create administrative structures that are capable of change and able to administer constantly changing environmental problems.[26] International Environmental law seeks to find solutions to a litany of environmental problems such as global warming, depletion of the stratospheric ozone layer, loss of biological diversity, pollution of coastal waters, nuclear accidents, persistent organic pollutants, and acid rain amongst others that cause the degradation of the environment.[27]

The significance of preserving the environment around the globe has therefore gradually risen across decades. The successful negotiation of Multilateral and bilateral environmental treaties is an important step in environmental governance through the successful implementation at international, regional, and national levels and the basis of international environmental law across national and international borders. Environmental laws hence provide the basis for the protection and conservation of biodiversity through the formulation of principles objectives and standards for the sustainable use of environmental resources, the protection of the ozone layer, the implementation of policy reform to reduce the effects of climate change, the protection of marine life, the regulation of hazardous wastes and sound chemical management as well as the

[25]United Nations Environmental Programme. *Environmental Rule of Law: First Global Report.* UNEP,www.unep.org/resources/assessment/environmental-rule-law-first-global-.

[26]Koivurova, Timo. *Introduction to International Environmental Law.* Routledge, 2013. [27]Lomborg, Bjørn. *The Skeptical Environmentalist: Measuring the Real State of the World.* Cambridge: Cambridge University Press, 2001. (Preface).

criminalization and sanction of destructive action. These principles and regulations form the foundation of the rule of law that influences environmental policy.

1.10. HOW THE ENVIRONMENT INTERACTS WITH INTERNATIONAL LAW

Nearly all global and regional human rights bodies have considered the link between the environment, environmental degradation, the rule of law, and internationally guaranteed human rights. In most instances, the complaints brought have not been based upon a specific right to a safe and environmentally sound environment, but rather upon rights to life, property, health, information, and family and home life.[28] Environmental Law emerges from the cultural traditions and moral and religious values of a society that continue to impact the development of legal norms. In the context of environmental protection, cultures, religions and legal systems throughout the world contain elements that respect and seek to conserve the natural bases of life, maintaining concepts that can enhance and enrich the development of modern environmental law.[29]

1.11.OBJECTIVES OF INTERNATIONAL ENVIRONMENTAL LAW

As with all environmental regulations, international environmental law can only strive to control and minimize pollution damage. In the field of environmental law, the state as the sanctioning authority is, therefore, an integral stakeholder in environmental governance that is necessary for implementing and enforcing the imperative link between the rule of law and sustainable environmental management. The environment and the rule of law ultimately remain closely interlinked because of the significant utility of the environment upon the state, the lives of its people, and its resources. International Environmental Law also addresses the following issues

a) THE ARTICULATION AND EMPHASIS ON THE PROTECTION OF ENVIRONMENTAL RIGHTS.

International law is binding at the international level, and it is no defense to breach an international obligation that a state's domestic law differs or that the government of the state has failed to give effect to the international norm as It is not only enough to provide for a legal right i.e. the right to a clean and healthy environment wihout provisions on the protection of the same.[30] It is therefore significant that environmental policy, guidelines, and regulations protect the peaceable enjoyment of the right. The law similarly protects the rights across different jurisdictions. The constitution that forms the public law confers the right and accordingly delineates the remedies in case of

[28] Kiss, Alexandre, and Dinah Shelton. *Guide to International Environmental Law.* Page 240, paragraph 3.

[29] *United Nations Environment Programme. Judicial Handbook.* Page 4.

[30] *Vienna Convention on the Law of Treaties.* Article 27 and 46.

infringement. The law may also direct the legislative arms of government to legislate further and provide appropriate measures to actualize the enjoyment of the right. Under the Kenyan Public Law, for instance, the National assembly legislates on national matters whilst county assemblies legislate on matters relating to devolved units to counties.[31] The central legislative arm of government in Kenya has enacted sectoral environmental regulations guided by key provisions from the Kenyan constitution of 2010 as well as the Environmental management and coordination Act that embodies international Environmental principles. These provisions of law founded on principles of international environmental law provide requisite regulations and remedies in case of the infringement of individual rights. In Kenya's constitution, the right to a clean and healthy environment is a fundamental right entrenched in the bill of rights in compliance with international environmental law as articulated in the Rio- Declaration.

The constitution imposes a legal obligation upon the legislative arm of government to provide the Legislative and operational framework that actualizes the enforcement of duties and obligations from the state and private individuals, towards the environment. This is an essential feature that underpins the complex and sensitive nature of the environment, its proximity to human life in the features of the environment as well as other associated subjects of both scientific and legislative concern. The legislation on environmental law is summarily concerned with the following aspects.

b) **THE DELINEATION OF THE LIMITS AND THE SCOPE OF ENJOYMENT OF RIGHTS.**

Another significant role of international environmental law in the scope of environmental matters is the extent of the enjoyment of rights. International Environmental law provides guidelines as pertains to the conduct of states in their jurisdictions and the boundary between the peaceable and reasonable enjoyment of other nations' rights and the violation of other citizens' peace. This demarcation is in form of standard regulations and compliance requirements. The exploitation of a state's resources has the potential to infringe the sovereignty of other states due to the transboundary or Trans-frontier environmental impacts, many species of wild animals, birds, and fish migrate across boundaries, threatening to create interstate disputes over rights to them. International environmental law is important in avoiding conflict and managing transboundary resources. The principles of international environmental law such as the Stockholm Declaration are critical in balancing the rights and privileges of exercising state sovereignty with the obligation

---

[31]*The Constitution of Kenya 2010.* Sixth Schedule.

of controlling damage to the environment of other States and areas beyond the limits of national jurisdiction.[32]

International environmental law, therefore, delineates legal rights. This is important as the principles of law only apply and clarifies the boundaries within which these legal rights are exercised. The purpose of the law is to ensure that individuals in recognition of the right and privileges of others peaceably enjoy their rights without interference or disturbance. Legislation in that regard demarcates the permissible extent beyond which enjoyment infringes upon other people's peace.

C) THE PROHIBITION OF THE INFRINGEMENT OF ENVIRONMENTAL RIGHTS

International Environmental sanctions prohibit the infringement of rights. Breach of an international obligation, whether based on a treaty or customary international law, gives rise to certain automatic consequences, the first of which is an obligation to cease the breach and conform conduct to the law.[33]Under national law in Kenya, international law is recognized as a legitimate anchor of the rule of law to the extent the international order is not repugnant to the Kenyan constitution. International custom and treaty, therefore, form an integral section of the law in Kenya as well as across other national jurisdictions.[34]In Kenyan legislation, prohibitive provisions are anchored in the principles of the international environmental law such as the precautionary principle and the polluter pays principle, these provisions sanction conduct that infringes upon the environmental right and provides penal sanctions for violation. Penal sanctions may be in the form of monetary fines as well as prison terms. This concept emanates from the endorsement of the force of law and the enforcement by a sovereign authority. This way it is possible to regulate and control human conduct.

d.) THE EMPHASIS ON STATUTORY REMEDIES FOR INFRINGEMENT OF RIGHTS.

International Environmental law seeks a cure to a legal right upon infringement. International Environmental law emphasizes the need for the legislative guideline to include legal remedies for the infringement of legal rights. Legal remedies seek to redress, recompense as well as mitigate deleterious action. Most legal remedies in environmental jurisprudence aim at environmental restoration as well as the compensation of victims of infringement. The law is also rife and

---

[32]Kiss, Alexandre, and Dinah Shelton. *Guide to International Environmental Law*. Page 12, paragraph 2.

[33]*La Grande Case (Germany v. United States)*, 2001 ICJ (June 27), 40 ILM 1069 (2001).

[34]Article 70 of the Kenyan constitution of 2010

conscious of the peculiar nature of environmental rights. The evolution of the law of torts has fashioned some extraordinarily peculiar concepts like the law on strict and absolute liability in some jurisdictions which require high thresholds and specific standards of care to minimize unforeseen conduct that may infringe upon environmental rights.

e) THE REQUIREMENT FOR INSTITUTIONAL FRAMEWORKS FOR THE ENFORCEMENT OF RIGHTS.

International Environmental law is based on the concept of rights and duties that confers obligations upon subjects. The state must nevertheless enforce the regulation as a sovereign power. The inability of laws and regulations to self-enforce necessitates the creation of agencies and authorities that enforce compliance or adherence. This is only possible through monitoring mechanisms that enable the determination of claims of infringement as well as intended infringement. The authorities provided in the law possess the authority of the state to enforce statutory compliance. The authorities and agencies under Kenyan law are mainly regulated by acts of parliament.

f) FRAMEWORK FOR THE ENFORCEMENT OF ENVIRONMENTAL STANDARDS.

International Environmental law emphasizes the need for a uniform application of various measures and regulations is important in the enforcement of environmental standards across jurisdictions and the accomplishment of the principles of equity, fairness, and compliance in environmental justice. The effectiveness of Environmental law in the application of sanctions and the recognition of individual rights is a concrete pillar in the quest for environmental justice. Environmental standards in a robust environmental legislative regime are especially an important step in the realization of sustainable development goals.

1.12. THE NECESSITY OF INTERNATIONAL ENVIRONMENTAL LAW.

The emergence of international environmental law required a change in human consciousness, an increased value placed on the environment, and concern about its destruction.[35]Not so long ago, international environmental law was considered a narrow specialty within the general field of international law. But today international environmental law has become a field in its own right, with subspecialties in wildlife law, marine pollution, freshwater resources, climate change, sustainable development, chemicals, and so forth.[36] International Environmental Law aims at addressing various dimensions of environmental challenges by investigating the causes of these problems, identifying what can be done to solve these challenges as well as examining what role the law can play in doing so. These are the fundamental questions of international environmental law.[37]A) Preventing transboundary environmental problems

In a practical sense International environmental law seeks to find ways for sovereign states to prevent transboundary environmental problems or to administer shared ecosystems jointly, this is because of the tension created by the fact that classical international law guarantees legislative and enforcement powers to territorial political communities, the boundaries of which are artificial from the perspective of pollution or natural ecosystems.[38]International environmental law, as a distinctive enterprise, seeks to promote cooperation among states to achieve joint gains. Classical International law, by contrast, focused on coexistence rather than cooperation by demarcating the respective jurisdiction of states hence failing to address the transboundary problem from the territorial and political perspective as environmental

problems have no respect for territorial borders.[39] International environmental law plays a crucial role in preventing transboundary environmental problems by providing a framework for cooperation, establishing standards, and facilitating diplomatic efforts among nations. Some of the key aspects of the role of international environmental law in preventing transboundary pollution include the following;

---

[35]Sachs, Aron. *The Humboldt Current: Nineteenth-Century Exploration and the Roots of American Environmentalism.* New York: Viking, 2006.).

[36] Bodansky, Daniel. *The Art and Craft of International Environmental Law.* Harvard University Press, 2010.

[37] Kronman, Anthony T. *Max Weber.* Stanford, CA: Stanford University Press, 1983.

[38]Koivurova, Timo. Introduction to International Environmental Law. Page 2.

[39]Croxton, Derek. "The Peace of Westphalia of 1648 and the Origins of Sovereignty." *The International History Review,* vol. 21, no. 3, Sep. 1999, pp. 569-591.

1) SETTING INTERNATIONAL STANDARDS

International environmental agreements establish standards and guidelines for sustainable practices and pollution control. Treaties such as the Basel Convention on Hazardous Wastes and the Paris Agreement on climate change provide benchmarks for countries to follow, ensuring that environmental regulations are aligned internationally.

2) PROMOTING COOPERATION AND INFORMATION SHARING

International environmental law encourages collaboration between nations. Countries are urged to share information about potential environmental threats, such as pollution or endangered species, facilitating early warning systems and coordinated responses. Bilateral and multilateral agreements foster communication and joint efforts to address shared environmental challenges.

3)PREVENTING TRANSBOUNDARY POLLUTION

Treaties and conventions specifically address issues of transboundary pollution, ensuring that pollutants do not harm neighboring countries. Agreements like the International Convention for the Prevention of Pollution from Ships (MARPOL) set regulations to prevent marine pollution, while the Convention on Long-Range Transboundary Air Pollution addresses air pollution crossing borders.

4)DISPUTE RESOLUTION

International environmental law provides mechanisms for resolving disputes between countries regarding transboundary environmental issues. International courts and tribunals, such as the International Court of Justice, offer platforms for countries to resolve conflicts related to shared resources or environmental damage.

5) CAPACITY BUILDING AND TECHNICAL ASSISTANCE

International agreements often include provisions for capacity building and technical assistance to help developing nations implement environmentally friendly policies and practices. This support helps countries prevent transboundary problems by strengthening their regulatory frameworks and enforcement capabilities.

6)PROMOTING CORPORATE RESPONSIBILITY

International environmental law encourages responsible behavior from multinational corporations operating across borders. Treaties often outline guidelines for corporate practices, ensuring that companies consider environmental impacts and adhere to international standards, reducing the likelihood of cross-border environmental damage.

1.13.THE DEEPWATER HORIZON OIL SPILL IN THE GULF OF MEXICO IN 2010

One notable real case of transboundary pollution is the Deepwater Horizon oil spill, which occurred in the Gulf of Mexico in 2010. Operated by British Petroleum (BP), the offshore drilling rig suffered a blowout, leading to a massive release of crude oil into the Gulf of Mexico over a period of 87 days. The spill is considered one of the largest environmental disasters in U.S. history and had severe ecological, economic, and social impacts on the surrounding areas. The spill contaminated the waters and coastlines of several U.S. states, including Louisiana, Mississippi, Alabama, Florida, and Texas, but the oil also drifted across international boundaries. Oil slicks reached as far as the shores of Mexico and Cuba, causing extensive damage to marine life, coastal ecosystems, and local economies. The spill had devastating effects on the fishing industry, tourism, and the livelihoods of communities' dependent on the Gulf's resources. The Deepwater Horizon oil spill highlights the challenges associated with transboundary pollution, emphasizing the need for international cooperation, stringent regulations, and effective response mechanisms to address environmental disasters that cross national borders. The explosion of BP's Deepwater Horizon offshore drilling unit in April 2010 led to a substantial oil spill in the Gulf of Mexico, causing far-reaching ecological, social, and economic repercussions. Gaining a comprehensive understanding of the spill's impacts is a complex task, requiring years of assessment due to the prolonged and evolving nature of its effects. Some consequences might persist or worsen over time, while others may not have fully manifested yet. Moreover, the spill's effects can be intertwined with other risk factors like climate change, fisheries, commercial shipping, military activities, and coastal development, making it challenging to isolate and assess the spill's specific impact. Marine mammals are particularly vulnerable to oil spills, facing direct harm through contact, inhalation, or ingestion of oil. Additionally, they can suffer injuries and disturbance from response activities, leading to further distress. The spill's aftermath may also cause long-term ecological changes, affecting the habitats and food sources of marine mammals.[40]

---

[40]Marine Mammal Commission. "Assessing the Long-term Effects of the BP Deepwater Horizon Oil Spill on Marine Mammals in the Gulf of Mexico." August 2011, https://www.mmc.gov/wp- content/uploads/ longterm_effects_bp_oilspil.pdf

1.14. THE SHELL BP GAS POLLUTION CASE, ALSO KNOWN AS THE BODO OIL SPILLS.

The Shell BP gas pollution case, also known as the Bodo oil spills, involves a protracted legal battle between the Nigerian communities of Bodo and the oil giants Shell and BP. The case centers around devastating oil spills that occurred in 2008 and 2009 in the Niger Delta region, causing significant environmental damage and adversely affecting the livelihoods of thousands of local residents. The spills were a result of pipeline failures, leading to the release of a massive volume of crude oil into the creeks and farmlands, severely impacting fishing and farming activities, which are the primary sources of income for the local communities.

The legal dispute intensified as the affected communities, supported by environmental groups, accused Shell and BP of negligence and demanded compensation for the environmental destruction and economic losses. After years of legal battles, in 2015, Shell agreed to pay £55 million (approximately $83 million) in compensation to the affected communities, marking one of the largest environmental settlements in Nigerian history. Additionally, as part of the settlement, both Shell and BP committed to cleaning up the affected areas and implementing measures to prevent future oil spills, emphasizing the need for corporate accountability and environmental responsibility.

Shell has acknowledged its responsibility for the aforementioned spills, but the company contends that the volume of oil spilled was approximately 4,000 barrels, affecting only 36 hectares of land. The pipelines belonging to the Shell Petroleum Development Company (SPDC) in the Bodo area are nearly half a century old, and they have not been adequately maintained or inspected by SPDC. Alarmingly, both spills continued to release oil into the environment for several weeks, even after SPDC had been made aware of the incidents. This situation raises concerns about the effectiveness of monitoring, maintenance practices, and timely response measures, highlighting the need for improved corporate responsibility and environmental stewardship in the oil industry.[41]

This case highlighted the severe environmental consequences of oil exploration and production in the Niger Delta and brought attention to the social and economic injustices faced by local communities. It also underscored the importance of stringent regulations, corporate accountability, and community engagement in the oil industry to prevent similar ecological disasters and ensure the protection of human rights and the environment in vulnerable regions.

---

[41]Leigh Day. "Oil Spills on the Niger Delta." Leigh Day, https://www.leighday. co.uk/news /cases- and-testimonials/cases/shell-bodo/.

B) ADDRESSING THE PROBLEM OF GLOBAL WARMING AND THE GREENHOUSE EFFECT.

Global warming and climate change are major Environmental issues. "Climate change," is used as a term to describe the change of climate attributed directly or indirectly to a human activity whose consequence alters the composition of the global atmosphere.[42] The term greenhouse effect is derived from the structure and function of greenhouses, also called a glass house, which allows the Penetration of radiation to warm it. Gases capable of absorbing radiant energy are called greenhouse gases (GHG). Greenhouses are used to grow flowers, vegetables, fruits, and tobacco throughout the year in a warm, agreeable climate. Similarly, there is a phenomenon called the "natural greenhouse" effect upon then Earth which enables the regulation of ideal temperatures that make the earth habitable to humans and biodiversity.[43] The purpose of climate change mitigation is to enact measures to limit the extent of climate change. Climate change mitigation can make a difference.[44] The climate is governed by natural influences, yet human activities have an impact on it as well. The main impact that humans exert on the climate is via the emission of greenhouse gases. Deforestation is another example of an activity that influences the climate.[45]

c) ADDRESSING ISSUES ABOUT THE SUSTAINABLE EXPLOITATION OF NATURAL RESOURCES

The continuous exploitation of natural resources poses significant environmental challenges and consequences; one major challenge is the sustainability of the exploitation of resources. This is coupled with continually increasing population pressure on the existing resources as well as uncontrolled exploitation that is likely to degrade the environment. The unregulated exploitation of forest resources and land amongst other environmental resources portends serious environmental issues such as soil erosion, desertification, loss of biological diversity as well as increased acidification of soil through farming activity. The author of the book 'The Last Tree,' outlines a vivid dissection of the social dysfunction and forest destruction in South and Southeast Asia. The author of the last tree explains the tragedy of environmental degradation reminiscent of Asia and other places where populations and industrialists mindlessly exploit forest resources

[42] Kiss, Alexandre, and Dinah Shelton. *Guide to International Environmental Law*. Page 11, paragraph 3.

[43] Karl, T.R., and Trenberth, K.E. "Modern Global Climate Change." *Science*, vol. 302, no. 5651, 2003, pp. 1719-1723. doi:10.1126/science.1090228.

[44] The International Energy Association IEA 2009

[45] The Essential Principles of Climate Literacy. "Climate.gov, https://www.climate. gov/ Teaching/ climate#:~:text=Essential%20Principle%206%3A %20Human%20activities,impacts%2 0throughout

%20the%20Earth%20system.

without consideration leaving local populations poor and embroiled in the continuous cycle of poverty. The author explains the tragedy of the haste to obtain development capital from wood- hungry countries, which has led to the issue of concessions to multinational companies on large forest areas.[46]

The timber concessionaires and the government exclude indigenous peoples and local forest-dependent villagers from the forest and its products, forcing the people to work for wages in the forest while forcing others to move into more remote parts of natural forests. Timber concessionaires make huge profits from the products of the forest, without regard to regenerating the natural forest or paying the local people for the loss thereby accelerating the cycle of poverty and forest degradation. Such is the tragedy across many areas of the globe where natural resources are exploited and the ecosystems are continually unreasonably destroyed for selfish gains leaving a trail of destruction to both the environment and local populations. Such tragedies necessitate action and a system of laws and regulations to combat human activity in the destruction of the environment.

D) ADDRESSING ISSUES ABOUT DEPLETION OF THE STRATOSPHERIC OZONE LAYER.

The ozone layer is a protective shield that guards the earth against harmful ultraviolet radiation that's detrimental to human life as well as to the survival of other species of biodiversity. The excessive release of chlorofluorocarbon gases commonly denoted as (CFCs) finally gets deposited into the stratosphere where constant and continued contact with the ozone layer releases chlorine gas which breaks down the ozone layer. International Environmental law seeks to strengthen global legislative infrastructure and action that is aimed at promoting appropriate measures and activity to prevent harmful activity to the ozone layer. The Vienna Convention proposes cooperation amongst states in research and scientific assessments of the problem of the deterioration of the ozone. [47]

E)ADDRESSING ISSUES ON LOSS OF BIOLOGICAL DIVERSITY

The loss of biodiversity is of great risk and consequence to both humans and the environment. This is because biodiversity sustains life on the planet through the interdependence of diverse species. Human activity and pollution of habitats are greatly responsible for the loss of biodiversity. The

[46]Diamond, Jared. *The Last Tree on Easter Island*. Penguin Classics, 2021.

[47] Brown Weiss, Edith. "International Environmental Law: Contemporary Issues and the Emergence of a New World Order" (1993). *Georgetown Law Faculty Publications and Other Works*, paper 1628.

interaction of humans with other living organisms has been the subject of discussion, debate, and regulation throughout history. A belief in human dominion over the earth and all its living resources led many to see other species as having only utilitarian value.[48] International environmental law seeks to bolster conservation efforts through legislative infrastructure.

F) ADDRESSING ISSUES ON POLLUTION OF COASTAL WATERS.

Harmful substances from the land such as plastic garbage, pesticides, oil spillages, phosphates from fertilizers, animal matter, human waste, and other pollutants from human activity are responsible for the contamination of coastal waters. These pollutants are responsible for the degradation of coastal waters as well as the loss of aquatic biodiversity. International Environmental law seeks to influence the legal infrastructure and policies in the management of contaminants as well as other degrading activities that contribute to pollution.

G)ADDRESSING ISSUES ON NUCLEAR ACCIDENTS.

Nuclear accidents have seriously negative and detrimental consequences on the environment such as nuclear radiation which can alter genetic matter besides causing serious health complications for humans. Nuclear accidents pollute the environment by emitting significant quantities of harmful radiation that takes many years to decay from the environment thereby polluting water, and soil and causing health consequences. Nuclear power plants must operate in the most secure manner respecting all safety measures and principles adopted at national, regional, and international levels. When safety measures and principles are ignored or are not properly observed by nuclear plant operators, a nuclear accident can occur with serious consequences for the environment, human health, and public opinion[49]

H)ADDRESSING ISSUES ON PERSISTENT ORGANIC POLLUTANTS

Persistent Organic Chemicals are also known as 'Forever chemicals'. These are poisonous chemical substances with having serious health consequences on human health. The effects of persistent organic pollutants are magnified by the fact that they are easily transported around the world through air and water thereby affecting humans and wildlife far away from their states of origin. Most organic pollutants are environmentally persistent and accumulate by passing from species to species through the food chain.

[48] Kiss, Alexandre, and Dinah Shelton. *Guide to International Environmental Law.* Page 176, paragraph 2.
[49] Pedraza, Jorge Morales. "World Major Nuclear Accidents and Their Negative Impact on The Environment, Human Health, And Public Opinion." *IJEEE*, vol. 21, no. 2, ISSN: 1054-853X.

A.)A MORAL OR ETHICAL OBLIGATION?

From the analysis of the uninterrupted African way of life in our traditional societies, the existing socio-economic patterns that existed were non-capitalistic basic setups. The interdependence of these traditional setups with the environment was a mutually beneficial one that provided a source of life and sustenance to populations. The preservation of the environment meant survival for these societies.

The concept of environmental conservation is therefore ancient and precedes the organization of modern society. Ancient societies recognized the obligation to preserve the environment as a moral and spiritual obligation evidenced by nature worshippers and reverence for holy spots in the forest ecosystems.[50]Environmental conservation is therefore an ancient idea that transcends the organization of society, perhaps out of indications that the earliest conservation efforts were borne out of a moral and spiritual obligation rather than a sanction by law, while traditional and ancient societies held the environment in high esteem, it was so because of the religious and moral considerations. Arguably today under international relations as pertains to organized political societies, Environmental conservation, regulation, and preservation is by dint amoral and ethical obligation. There is an ever-increasing consciousness of the utility, interdependence, and fragility of the environment as a habitat, ecological anchor, and cultural repository.

B.)AN INDIVIDUAL OR COLLECTIVE OBLIGATION?

International environmental problems typically require ongoing management rather than merely an adjudication of the rights and responsibilities of the parties. It requires cooperation rather than merely coexistence among states.[51] The obligation towards preserving and protecting the environment is collective and universal as environmental benefits and liabilities are common and transboundary. There is a collective duty amongst the members of nations that form the fabric of our society to protect and conserve the environment, these obligations emanate from individual rights. Environmental problems have, as a general rule, transboundary effects. Therefore, states realized early that cooperation, common rules, and standards are better than unilateral action. The outcome of cooperation in the environmental field can be seen in the number and quality of treaties and other instruments that have been put in place for the protection of the environment.[52] Many

---

[50] UNESCO. "Mijikenda Kaya Forests." UNESCO World Heritage Centre, whc.unesco.org/en/list/1231.

[51]Bodansky, Daniel. *The Art and Craft of International Environmental Law.* Page 22, paragraph 3.

[52] United States General Accounting Office (GAO), International Agreements Are Not Well Monitored (GAO-RCED-92–43, 1992).

environmental problems transcend national boundaries and interests, necessitating a coordinated global effort. This is particularly true in areas outside national authority, and where there is transboundary pollution on land and in the oceans, atmosphere, and outer space.[53]The need to regulate human activity toward the environment requires the implementation of positive sanctions and guidelines for regulating individual and collective action to meet these demands. Environmental law in this sense encompasses the framework for positive, prohibited, and remedial action towards the enforcement of obligations.

1.15. THE BASIC PRINCIPLES OF INTERNATIONAL ENVIRONMENTAL REGULATION.

International environmental law operates at many levels: Transboundary, global, domestic, or an amalgam of the three. Firstly, there are Transboundary problems such as air and water pollution or the protection of migratory species which are not respecters of artificial state boundaries.[54] International law is founded on many foundational principles that have particular significance in the development of international environmental law. The United Nations Charter sets out those principles deemed to be of constitutional importance to the United Nations member states in Article 2.[55] They include sovereign equality, good faith compliance with agreements to which a state is a party, cooperation in addressing matters of international concern, non-interference in the domestic affairs of states, and peaceful settlement of international disputes. Most importantly the charter sets out the concept of state sovereignty.[56]

The concept of legislation on environmental matters has evolved around these principles to enhance the regulation of human behavior and the formulation of progressive standards to govern the preservation of the environment. These principles are therefore significant and necessary in the implementation of the principles of good governance that relate to human action and behavior and the consequences of such effects, upon the environment and other humans.

A.) SOVEREIGN EQUALITY AND SOVEREIGNTY OF THE STATE OVER NATURAL RESOURCES AND WEALTH.

The Preamble to the Biodiversity Convention affirms that the conservation of biological diversity is a common concern of humankind', that states have 'sovereign rights over their biological resources, and that they are 'responsible for conserving their biological diversity and for

[53]Langkawi Declaration on the Environment.

[54] Nagtzaam, Gerry, Evan van Hook, and Douglas Guilfoyle. *International Environmental Law: A Case Study Analysis*. Page 2.

[55]*The United Nations Charter.* Article 2.

[56]Kiss, Alexandre, and Dinah Shelton. *Guide to International Environmental Law.* Page 11, paragraph 3.

sustainably using their biological resources.[57]The principle appreciates the principle of sovereignty of each state over its environment and its natural resources as a matter of right. States hence have, by the Charter of the United Nations and the principles of international law, the sovereign right to exploit their resources according to their environmental policies.[58] Environmental law concerns itself with the evolution of sound principles of the preservation and exploitation of states' resources. These principles are founded in private international law as well as public law.

B.)'EQUITY' AND 'IN ACCORDANCE WITH COMMON BUT DIFFERENTIATED RESPONSIBILITIES

In line with the Rio Declaration and view of the different contributions to global environmental degradation, States have common but differentiated responsibilities. Specifically, developed countries should acknowledge the responsibility they bear in the international pursuit of sustainable development because of the pressures their societies place on the global environment and of the technologies and financial resources they command.[59]Environmental obligations arise out of rights and duties, while environmental consciousness is diverse across jurisdictions and non- obligatory, there is a universally recognized duty to maintain a clean and healthy environment among civilized nations. This consensus across nations on the need to protect the environment and observe collective obligations has borne the international agenda that informs our discussion. The need arises out of the understanding that a failure to limit persistent deleterious action may ultimately lead to irreversible consequences that affect the planet and human life directly. The obligation requires individuals to consciously adhere to, promote and reflect upon the positive efforts that contribute directly to the maintenance of a clean and healthy environment as well as the avoidance of the undesirable and deleterious activities that comprise the enjoyment of this right by other people.

Article 3 of The 1992 Climate Change Convention sets out 'Principles' aimed at guiding state parties. The principles are significant in achieving the objective and implementation of the provisions of the Convention. The obligation of parties to protect the climate system is 'based on equity' and 'in accordance with their common but differentiated responsibilities and respective capabilities following which developed country parties should take the lead.[60]

---

[57] *Convention on Biological Diversity.* Preamble. 1992.
[58]*The Stockholm Declaration on the Human Environment.* Principle 21. 1972.
[59]*The Rio Declaration on Environment and Development.* Principle 7. 1992.
[60]*The United Nations Framework Convention on Climate Change.* Article 3. 1992..

C.) GOOD FAITH COMPLIANCE WITH AGREEMENTS TO WHICH A STATE IS A PARTY.

In the law-making process of international Environmental Law, after a convention is signed, it enters into a process of ratification. This means that states must ask their legislative organs e.g. Parliament to adopt the convention and incorporate it into the domestic legal order. Unless a state ratifies a convention, the convention does not have binding effects on that state.[61]In the framework model of environmental legislation, policymakers have taken an affirmative approach through positive regulations that embody the concept of positive action, examples include undertakings by citizens to promote remedial action in form of afforestation, restoration of degraded environments, protection of catchment areas, and the preservation of endangered species. This approach by way of collective positive action is important in the ultimate regeneration of natural ecosystems across jurisdictions. Affirmative policies and legislations are manifest in both public and private law. The Kenyan constitution for instance affirms the right to a clean environment in the provisions of article 42, of the constitution that forms the bill of rights.[62] Kenya's constitution also places an obligation upon the state to maintain the country's national tree cover at not less than 10 percent. This affirmative provision is based upon the scientific basis of the progressive reduction of the global carbon footprint as well as the maintenance of global forest cover for the benefit of citizens.

D.) COOPERATION IN ADDRESSING MATTERS OF INTERNATIONAL CONCERN.

Article 12 (1) of the convention highlights the need for state Parties to recognize everyone's right to the enjoyment of the highest attainable standard of physical and mental health and the obligation of states to take steps including the improvement of all aspects of environmental and industrial hygiene. Without impairing the inherent right of all peoples to enjoy and utilize fully and freely their natural wealth and resources.[63] States cooperate in improving the state of the environment in various ways most importantly through legislation. In the scope of regulation, there is a manifestation of Prohibitive regulations that sanction negative action and impose punitive consequences. These sanctions are particularly important in accentuating the power of the state and sovereignty over natural resources as well as enforcing environmental rights and obligations. Most model environmental legislations such as Acts of Parliament prohibit acts that violate or infringe upon other people's right to enjoy a clean and healthy environment and discourage avoidable deleterious actions such as indiscriminate pollution patterns and degradation of

[61]Louka, Elli. *International Environmental Law.* Page 18, paragraph 3.

[62] *The Constitution of Kenya.* Article 42.

[63]Article 12 Ibid

ecosystems. Most of these legislations regulate activities of international concern such as mining and natural resource protection, wildlife conservation, Water pollution control, and general Environmental Management for the peaceful enjoyment of the right to a clean and healthy environment.

D.) NON-INTERFERENCE IN THE DOMESTIC AFFAIRS OF STATES.

Three fundamental pillars augment the character and foundations of the modern state; they include a territory, a population, and a sovereign power in the form of government. State sovereignty is one of the oldest principles of international law. Sovereignty accords every state exclusive, legislative, judicial, and executive jurisdiction over activities on its territory. Subject to compliance with international law.[64] International environmental law is a branch of public international law that is a body of law created by States for States to govern problems that arise between States. In the attempt to control pollution and the depletion of natural resources within a framework of sustainable development. Though, nations must uphold the rule of law and desist from interfering with the socio-economic, cultural, or political affairs of other countries.[65] Under national jurisdictions where the Legislative authority lies in the domain of the legislative organs of government such as the executive, the legislature, and the judiciary. These organs of state play a significant role in shaping and implementing the principles of international environmental law and policy at the national level. International Environmental law emphatically buttresses the very key objectives of international law as pertains to non-interference in the domestic affairs of states

E.) PEACEFUL SETTLEMENT OF INTERNATIONAL DISPUTES.

The peaceful settlement of international disputes is recognized as a basic method and principle that governs the settlement of international disputes amongst states. The Charter of the United Nations requires state parties to resolve all disputes through peaceful means.[66] International environmental law as entrenched in the basic principles of legislation, especially under state obligations emphasizes this responsibility as a means of promoting international cooperation and harmony in environmental matters.

---

[64]Kiss, Alexander, and Dinah Shelton. *Guide to International Environmental Law*. Page 11, paragraph 3.

[65]The Vietnamese Ministry of Natural Resources and Environment, Department of Legal Affairs Handbook, titled International Environmental Law: Multilateral Environmental Agreements, Page 10, Paragraph 1.

[66] United Nations Charter. Art. 2, para. 3.

CHAPTER 2

THE DEVELOPMENT OF INTERNATIONAL ENVIRONMENTAL LAW TRACING THE EVOLUTION OF INTERNATIONAL ENVIRONMENTAL LAW ACROSS NATIONAL FRONTIERS

2.0. THE GENESIS OF INTERNATIONAL ENVIRONMENTAL LAW.

The development and evolution of international environmental law is part of a greater transformation of the subject of international law in the context of inter-state and cross-boundary cooperation for the achievement of social-economic welfare and development of economic and the common interest of humankind in protecting the natural environment.67 Many people make a general assumption about the character of international environmental law without giving serious thought to its history and character. It is tempting to think that international Environmental law is and always has been a sham.68 The genesis of international environmental law can be traced back to the mid-20th century when the world began to recognize the urgent need for coordinated efforts to address environmental challenges on a global scale. In the 1960s, concerns arose regarding specific areas such as cultural heritage preservation, declining tuna stocks, endangered species protection, and wetland conservation. During this period, international agreements and conventions, such as the Ramsar Convention on Wetlands and the Convention on International Trade in Endangered Species, were established to tackle these issues and promote the responsible use of natural resources.

As environmental awareness deepened in the 1970s and 1980s, the focus of international environmental law broadened to encompass interconnected biological diversity, spanning various sectors including species conservation, climate change mitigation, ecosystem preservation, and sustainable management of water and land resources. This shift in perspective led to the creation of more comprehensive and far-reaching conventions, such as the Convention on Biological Diversity and the United Nations Framework Convention on Climate Change. These agreements laid the foundation for a more holistic approach to environmental protection, acknowledging the interdependence of ecosystems and the need for international cooperation to address pressing environmental issues. Through these developments, the genesis of international environmental law

---

[67]Bernie, Patricia, Alan Boyle, and Catherine Redgwell. *International Law and the Environment.* 3rd ed., Oxford University Press, 2009.

[68]Brierly, J.L. *The Outlook for International Law.* Oxford at the Clarendon Press, 1944.

marked a crucial step towards fostering global collaboration and shared responsibility in safeguarding the planet's natural heritage. The international environmental movement has thereafter been instrumental in opposing unregulated economic development by emphasizing the need for sustainable environmental management and economic development centered on quality life and a clean environment.

2.01. THE HISTORICAL DEVELOPMENT OF INTERNATIONAL ENVIRONMENTAL LAW.

Environmental conservation and protection have gained impetus as one of the most significant concerns in the global community. Human activity continually causes environmental degradation at an extraordinary pace, it is, therefore, important to put this phenomenon in check to prevent the likelihood causation of permanent and irreversible damage.[69] The subject of codified Environmental law was non-existent in many states before the introduction of codified rules, nevertheless principles of environmental conservation and the preservation of biodiversity thrived in many tribal cultures as either ethical, moral, or spiritual obligations towards the environment. There still exist common rules relating to environmental management in many agrarian, nomadic, and natural resource-reliant communities which engage in activities such as fishing and gathering, these common rules govern some aspects of the environment.

The edict of colonization through colonial regimes in many developing and underdeveloped countries however introduced an interesting aspect of regulation in codified environmental Legislation in most developing countries, these developments have played an interesting and extraordinary role in shaping the constituent legal regimes governing the management and exploitation of environmental resources and biodiversity.

2.02. STAGES IN THE DEVELOPMENT OF INTERNATIONAL ENVIRONMENTAL LAW.

Environmental activists and lobby groups have continually put pressure on state governments in developed countries to implement rigorous policies in a bid to reduce pollution, environmental degradation, and destruction of natural resources such as water sources and forests.[70] These continuous efforts over time have evolved a set of internationally accepted principles that form the crux and substratum of international environmental law. The documented Evolution of international environmental law can be classified and distinguished by the three periods of

---

[69] Shelton, Dinah, and Alexandre Charles Kiss. *Judicial Handbook on Environmental Law*. Introduction by Hon. Judge Christopher G. Weeramantry. UNEP, 2005.

[70] Elli Louka, 'Introduction to International Environmental Law,' page 18, Para.

transformation notably three major 'periods.[71] The period until about 1970 may be referred to as the traditional era, while the subsequent period preceding the 1972 United Nations Conference on the Human Environment that was held in, Stockholm to the 1992 UN Conference on Environment and Development in Rio de Janeiro (UNCED) Stockholm is referred to the 'modern era and the 'post-modern era' that extends from Rio onwards.[72]

2.03.THE TRADITIONAL ERA.

One of the earliest conventions on the Environment is The Convention for the Protection of Birds Useful to Agriculture which came into force in 1902. It is one of the pioneer global conventions that entered into force to protect specific wildlife species. The Convention was specifically designated to promote the conservation of bird species that were considered valuable in promoting agricultural activities and products such as insectivores.[73] Other early boundary water treaties in a bid to deal with Transboundary water pollution and quality standards contained measures to reduce and prevent water pollution.[74] Another notable legislation before the Stockholm Conference is the Convention Relative to the Preservation of Fauna and Flora in their Natural State largely applied to Africa.[75] The Convention Relating to the Preservation of Fauna and Flora in their Natural State in 1933 is among the earliest international conventions adopted for the protection of biodiversity in Africa. The convention presents many similarities with the exclusionary conservation conventions adopted in later years across the globe.

The preamble of the convention underlines that "the natural fauna and flora of certain parts of the world, and in particular Africa, are in danger, in present conditions, of extinction and permanent injury." According to the framers of the convention, the preservation of natural resources is achievable through the delineation of special conservation areas and the strict enforcement of regulations.

The Convention on Nature Protection and Wildlife Preservation in the Western

[71]Edith Brown Weiss, 'The Evolution of International Environmental Law' Japanese Yearbook of International Law, 54 (2011): 1.

[72]Peter H Sand 'Origin and History in 'The Oxford Handbook of International Environmental Law,' Page 50.

[73]The 1902 Convention for the Protection of Birds Useful to Agriculture (Paris, Mar. 19, 1902) [74]The treaties entered between the United States and Canada include the United States-Canada Agreement Regarding the Establishment of Joint Pollution Contingency Plans for pollution from Oil and Other Noxious Substances (June 19, 1974), 25 UST 1280, TIAS 7861; United States- Canada Agreement on Great Lakes Water Quality with Annexes (Nov. 22, 1978), 30 U.S.T. 1383, TIAS No. 9257, amended Oct. 16, 1983, TIAS No. 10798.

[75]International Union for Conservation of Nature. "Convention relative to the Preservation of Fauna and Flora in their Natural State." IUCN, TRE-000069, 8 Nov. 1933.

Hemisphere is also another convention that considered the creation of specially designated areas such as reserves that would be utilized in the conservation and protection of wild animals and plants including migratory birds.[76]

2.04. THE IMPACT OF ENVIRONMENTAL REGULATIONS IN THE TRADITIONAL ERA.

1. THE INTRODUCTION OF STRICT ENVIRONMENTAL REGULATIONS

At the onset of the introduction of strict environmental regulations that carved out conservation areas such as wildlife reserves and animal parks, there was a strong feeling of resentment by local populations toward these alien and mysterious concepts. Indigenous Africans for instance detested these laws as the colonial masters imposed rules and regulations in the management of the environment that were strictly applied and enforced to conserve and protect such places that were naturally inhabited by wildlife and plant species though they were initially freely accessed and accessible areas that were utilized for hunting and gathering, collection of wood products such as firewood and timber, building as well as grazing grounds for agrarian and nomadic pastoralists. The introduction of environmental regulations grossly interfered with the natives' fashion and style of life.

2. THE ENFORCEMENT OF STRICT ENVIRONMENTAL REGULATIONS.

The introduction of environmental regulations and delineation of nature reserves from consumptive use marked the first significant step in the perpetration of environmental law in the first phase of the introduction of environmental regulations in Africa. Governing factions of traditional societies employed administrative and organizational abilities to harness the manual labor of the working masses by enslavement. This phenomenon expelled agrarian communities, who were dependent on natural resources such as forest resources, principally timber and wood from the forest, before proceeding on. The prevalent and constant conflict finally arose due to the continuous cycle of subjugation, oppression, exclusion, and exploitation leading to a revolt by the forest-dependent people. [77] These are among the earliest codified attempts to establish Environmental law in Africa.

---

[76]Convention on Nature Protection and Wildlife Preservation in the Western Hemisphere." 56 Stat. 1354. U.S. Fish and Wildlife Service.

[77] Introduction to World Forestry. Jack C. Westoby. Basil Blackwell. 1989.

3. INTRODUCTION OF NEW REGULATIONS CONCERNING THE HUNTING, KILLING, AND CAPTURING OF FAUNA

The convention proposed the establishment of regulations to check the, capturing hunting, and extermination of biodiversity outside protected areas, as well as the prohibition and control of the trafficking of game products such in the form of trophies, and the prohibition of certain methods of and weapons for the hunting, killing, capturing and destruction of biodiversity including wildlife.[78] The model of the convention has laid the foundation for the evolution of environmental law laws and regulations that embody the principles of sustainable development and conscionable exploitation of resources concerning the preservation of the natural environment.

4. CONSTITUTION OF SPECIAL AREAS AND DELINEATION OF SPECIAL AREAS REMOVED FROM CONSUMPTIVE USES.

The convention proposed the constitution and delineation of special areas removed from consumptive uses such as strict nature reserves, national parks, and other reserves. The state would limit and prohibit the extermination, collection, or destruction of flora and fauna hunting, killing, or capturing, of wildlife within such areas.[79] The earliest description of such special areas proposed to preserve areas containing predominantly unmodified natural systems, the delineation of such areas aims to facilitate long-term maintenance of existing biological diversity, and the provision of a sustainable flow of natural products and services to meet community needs.[80] The constitution of special areas was also important in protecting and maintaining the biological diversity and natural values of the delineated areas to promote sound management practices for sustainable production purposes in the long term, to protect the natural resource base from alienation for other land-use purposes that would be detrimental to biological diversity as well as to contribute to regional and national development.

---

[78] Preamble of the Convention Relative to the Preservation of Fauna and Flora in their Natural State." Enacted on 8 Nov. 1933, University of Oslo Library, www.jus.uio.no/english/services/library/treaties/06/6-02/preservation-fauna-natural.html. [79] Article 2 Preamble of the Convention Relative to the Preservation of Fauna and Flora in their Natural State." Enacted on 8 Nov. 1933, University of Oslo Library, www.jus.uio.no/english/services/library/treaties/06/6-02/preservation-fauna-natural.html. [80] Article 2 (2)Preamble of the Convention Relative to the Preservation of Fauna and Flora in their Natural State." Enacted on 8 Nov. 1933, University of Oslo Library, www.jus.uio.no/english/services/library/treaties/06/6-02/preservation-fauna- natural.htmlDefinition of natural reserves according to the convention on the Preservation of Fauna and Flora in their Natural State of 1933

Proposed special areas under the convention include;

I.)STRICT NATURE RESERVES.

These are areas that are specially protected and managed purposely for scientific reasons, the nature reserves are areas on land and sea. Strict Nature reserves have comparatively exceptional representative ecosystems alongside physiological features such as geological sites and animal species. These forms of biodiversity are important in scientific environmental monitoring and research.

Strict nature reserves are managed to promote the preservation of ecosystems, habitats, and species in an uninterrupted state to facilitate the continued preservation of genetic resources in a vibrant and evolutionary state, this is significant in maintaining established ecological processes, safeguarding structural landscape features or rock exposures, to secure examples of the natural environment for scientific studies, environmental monitoring and education, including baseline areas from which all avoidable access is excluded to minimize disturbance by careful planning and execution of research and other approved activities as well as to limit public access that may lead to interference.

II.) WILDERNESS AREAS.

These are majorly places on land or sea with very little modification or no modification at all. The main purposes of conserving these areas are to retain or ensure that they are protected to preserve their influence and natural character. This is important for future generations to experience and have an understanding and enjoyment of areas undisturbed by human action to maintain the essential natural attributes and qualities of the environment over the long term.[81]

III.) NATIONAL PARKS.

National Park areas are delineated majorly to facilitate the management, conservation, and preservation of ecosystems and recreation. National parks are natural areas of land or sea and are select areas where the protection of ecological of diverse ecosystems for sustainability purposes occurs. National parks have a variety of socio-economic significance, they provide a platform for scientific research, they are spiritually significant to many communities, and they provide recreational, spiritual, aesthetic utility, and visitor opportunities. These utilities must, however, conform to environmental conservation objectives as well as cultural compatibility. National parks provide representative examples of physiographic regions, for the enhancement and conservation

---

[81] UCN. "Protected Area Category." IUCN, https:// www.iucn.org/theme/protected-areas/our- work/ protected-area-categories.

of species, genetic resources as well as biotic communities, to which they sustain ecological stability amongst various species of biodiversity. Most importantly national parks eliminate and prevent destructive exploitation and occupation.

IV.) NATURAL MONUMENTS.

These are protected areas whose management is majorly for the protection and conservation of particular natural features. They normally contain either one or multiple, particularly natural or cultural features that contain exceptional or distinctive value because of the feature's intrinsic uncommonness, representative and aesthetic character, or cultural importance. Such features are managed to preserve in perpetuity particular extraordinary natural features for the reason that their natural significance, unique or, spiritual connotations, and representational quality.

V.) SPECIES MANAGEMENT AREAS.

This refers to a protected area managed purposely for the protection and preservation of biodiversity by way of management involvement. There is an active intervention to maintain habitats and achieve certain stipulations for specific species of biodiversity. These activities ensure that the management of such areas achieves the requisite conditions appropriate to protect important animal or biodiversity species, biotic communities, and groups of species. Species management areas may be delineated from particular physical features within the physical environs where it is established that such places require human intervention for the best possible biodiversity management. Such actions are critical in facilitating environmental monitoring and scientific research which is the basic actions linked to sustainable resource management. Species management areas also facilitate the development, conservation, and preservation of areas for public education and wildlife management which facilitate the eradication, misuse, or occupation that is detrimental to the main objectives conservation objectives of such designated places.

VI.) PROTECTED LANDSCAPE/SEASCAPE.

Protected Landscape/Seascape are protected and managed purposely to conserve and protect landscape or seascape for recreational and environmental reasons. The safeguarding of such areas arises out of the fact that human beings and the natural environment have interacted over long periods thereby creating extraordinary environs that occupy important ecological and aesthetic cultural values that contain diverse biological habitats with great biological diversity. It's of great significance to safeguard the integrity of the interaction between the environment and human beings because it is critical in the maintenance, protection, and evolution of the landscape. The objective of managing such areas facilitate the harmonious relationship between nature and cultural activity, especially by the management of building practices, traditional land uses, as well as social-cultural implications that augment economic lifestyles and activities which are harmonious with the preservation and conservation of the socio-cultural fabric of the surrounding communities as pertains to the preservation of the landscape and connected ecosystems and animal species and habitats. The protection of landscapes and seascapes also eliminates and averts inappropriate land-use patterns and activities. It also enhances recreational and aesthetic utilities for tourism purposes and promotes scientific and educational activity that contributes to the interests of adjacent populations such as economic and ecological benefits that enhance the welfare of local communities by way of natural products such as forest and fisheries products and services such as clean water or income from sustainable tourism.

VII.) MANAGED RESOURCE PROTECTED AREA.

This refers to areas protected and managed mainly for the sustainable use of natural Ecosystems.

2.05. THE DEVELOPMENT OF ENVIRONMENTAL LAW IN THE MODERN ERA.

The physical and legal borders between states are continuously and increasingly becoming irrelevant as they're being overridden by the human interface, this phenomenon has led to the development of new regulations that control and regulate the existing environmental relationships and issues that result in cross-boundary and intra boundary disputes. The dire need to regulate environmental issues has borne the negotiation and legislation of many treaties and conventions treaties that provide guidelines for cross-border environmental conduct.[82] The conservation efforts on a global scale commenced in the 1960s, focusing on safeguarding specific sectors like cultural heritage, declining tuna populations, endangered species, and wetlands. By the 1990s, the emphasis shifted to interconnected biological diversity spanning species, climate, ecosystems, water, and land. Conventions such as the Ramsar Convention on Wetlands, the World Heritage Convention, and the Convention on International Trade in Endangered Species were established in the 1970s, aiming to preserve and sustainably utilize specific natural resources. [83]The Stockholm Convention is among the earliest and distinctly notable instruments that laid the foundation in the scope of the evolution of environmental legislation, the international conference held in 1968 provided nations of the world an opportunity to examine the challenges associated with the

[82]Vietnamese Ministry of Natural Resources and Environment, Department of Legal Affairs. "International Environmental Law Multilateral Environmental Agreements." Page 10, para. 4 [83] Ministry of Natural Resources and Environment, Department of Legal Affairs. "International Environmental Law: Multilateral Environmental Agreements." International Publishing House, 2017, p. 27.

environment, the conference created the foundation for dialogue and deliberation on environmental issues as outlined in the agenda of the United Nations by emphasizing the contemplation of the significance of the problem by the international community through public opinion.[84]

The 1972 United Nations Stockholm Conference on the Human Environment (Stockholm Conference) and the 1992 Rio de Janeiro Conference on Environment and Development (Rio Conference) laid a new foundation for the international order for environmental law. The Stockholm and Rio conferences were significant path-breaking moments in the history of environmental jurisprudence. Their outcomes have been fundamental in laying significant progress in the development and implementation of international environmental law.[85]The General Assembly convened the 1972UN Conference on the Human Environment (Stockholm Conference), the 1992UN Conference on Environment and Development (UNCED, Rio Conference), and the 2002 World Summit on Sustainable Development (WSSD, Johannesburg Conference). All of these conferences are considered landmarks in the development of international environmental law.[86]

The principles outlined in the Stockholm Declaration (1972), further elaborated upon in the Rio Declaration on Environment and Development (1992), have significantly shaped the course of international environmental law over the past four decades. Regardless of their varying degrees of binding authority, these principles have served as a source of inspiration for the creation of new international legal norms. They have permeated numerous national legal systems and, at times, have subtly influenced decisions made by courts and tribunals, even when only implicitly referenced. These principles have played a pivotal role in guiding the structuring of laws amidst a swift and ongoing process of legal evolution.[87]

---

[84] U.N. F. COSOC, Annexes, Agenda Item 12 (Doc. E/4466/Add.$) at 2 (1968).

[85] The Evolution of International Environmental Law Edith Brown Weiss Georgetown University Law Center, weiss@law.georgetown.edu available online at https://scholarship. law. Georgetown. edu/facpub/1669/

[86] Elli Louka, International Environmental Law-Fairness, Effectiveness, and World Order, page 12.

[87] Yann Kerbrat, Sandrine Maljean-Dubois. The Role of International Law in the Promotion of the Precautionary Principle. Carina Costa de Oliveira, Gabriela G. B. Lima Moraes, Fabrício Ramos Ferreira (dir.), A interpretação do princípio da precaução no direito brasileiro, no direito comparado e no direito internacional, Pontes, pp. 275-284, 2019. ffhalshs-02342746f

2.06. THE IMPACT OF THE STOCKHOLM CONFERENCE ON THE DEVELOPMENT OF INTERNATIONAL ENVIRONMENTAL LAW AND POLICY.

One of the fundamental contributions of the Stockholm declaration to environmental governance is the universal recognition of the urgent need to provide a legal basis for the right to a healthy and wholesome environment that supports the enjoyment of human rights for the individual. The initial draft prepared by the committee was based on the acknowledgment of the right to an adequate environment for individuals and the obligation for states to take responsibility for damaging other states' environments outside national jurisdiction.[88] This was the first acknowledgment of innovative values to responsibility govern the relationship of the community of nations in the new era of environmental activism. This step also provided a crucial foundation in support of the institution and amplification of novel rules and regulations in international law as well as to conduct essential in giving effect to the values espoused in the Stockholm Declaration. [89]

The Stockholm declaration encloses common principles that enhance, guide, and motivate guide the global international society in preserving and enhancing the human environment. These principles include;

1. **THE UNIVERSAL RECOGNITION OF THE URGENT NEED TO PROVIDE A LEGAL BASIS FOR THE RIGHT TO A HEALTHY AND WHOLESOME ENVIRONMENT**

Environmental protection issues arising from international engagements community have been handled in the context of bilateral disputes resulting from Trans-Frontier Environmental degradation and pollution. There is a common understanding amongst members of the international community about the broad scope of environmental challenges, and the ineffectiveness of trying to solve environmental issues by use of regulations intended to solve mutual problems because they provide inadequate resolutions that transmit the ecological damage to different places.[90]

---

[88] United Nations. "Paragraph 77." Conference Document A/CONF.48/PC/57.

[89] Strong, Maurice F. Statement before the Second Committee of the General Assembly. 19 Oct. 1972, pp. 2-3. (Mimeo.)

[90]Kiss, Alexandre, and Dinah Shelton. Guide to International Environmental Law. Page 90, para. 1

2.Environmental management and Socio-economic development

The declaration emphasized the acknowledgment of the fact that environmental management and conservation is an important socio-economic aspect of the development of the human life and that the need to protect, preserve and improve the environment is a collective obligation of all governments and populations across the world, and that accordingly the extraordinary ability of human beings to transform the surrounding can stimulate socioeconomic benefits and progress for many people if prudently applied. The declaration pointed out the risk of uninhibited development to human life, health, and the environment.

3. ADDRESSING UNDER DEVELOPMENT AND ENVIRONMENTAL CHALLENGES

One of the major highlights of the declaration is that underdevelopment is a major cause of environmental problems in many countries because it deprives populations, of the right to access and afford proper food, sanitation, water, and other amenities, in this regard most environmental problems are connected to the effects technological advancement and industrialization.The appreciation of the common need for appropriate measures to mitigate the challenges caused by population pressure put upon the environment led to a consensus on the need to act collectively to preserve the environment and prohibit further destruction of the environment by endearing the common convictions that human beings have the fundamental right to freedom, equality, and enough conditions of wellbeing in a quality environment that sustains dignity.

4. ACKNOWLEDGMENT OF THE NEED TO PRESERVE AND PROTECT THE ENVIRONMENT.

In the same regard that there is an obligation to preserve, safeguard and enhance the state of the environment for the present and future generations. Policies that endorse discriminative and oppressive behavior including, racial discrimination and segregation, apartheid, and other forms of colonial and foreign domination stand condemned and be mandatorily abolished.

2.07. THE CONTRIBUTIONS OF THE STOCKHOLM CONVENTION TO INTERNATIONAL ENVIRONMENTAL LAW. EMPHASIS ON THE NEED FOR SUSTAINABLE PRESERVATION AND MANAGEMENT OF NATURAL RESOURCES.

The declaration underscores the obligation to preserve and protect the naturally occurring resources that include air, land, water, animals, and plants for the benefit of the present and future generations. In this regard, it is important to plan for and manage these resources carefully and prudently. The resources which cannot be renewed should be utilized sparingly to prevent their future depletion whilst benefits accruing from such resources should be prudently managed for the benefit of future generations.[91] This is achievable if mandatory initiatives are taken to restore and improve the ability of our planet to produce important renewable natural resources.[92] The human race is in an important place in the ecosystem as human beings are bestowed with an extraordinary obligation to protect and prudently manage the environment and its constituent heritage. Man has a special responsibility to safeguard and wisely take care of the wildlife and its heritage in its ecosystems and to ensure that during planning and development policy makers consider the significance of nature's conservation from destruction by multifarious social-economic factors.[93]

1. EMPHASIS ON THE NEED TO HALT DELETERIOUS AND HAZARDOUS ACTIVITIES TO THE ENVIRONMENT.

The declaration recognizes and highlights the challenges and the mess the inconsiderate release of excessive concentrations of harmful substances such as poisonous chemicals and excessive heat poses to human beings and the environment. The declaration, therefore, imposes an obligation upon states to discourage polluting activities upon the environment within national jurisdictions. It emphasizes the endorsement of proactive efforts and struggles against pollution to ensure that adverse permanent harm does not inflict upon ecosystems. To achieve these objectives states must take proactive steps to protect and prevent the contamination of seas by hazardous elements that pose a danger to human life and health, a hazard to aquatic life, and a potential impairment and destruction or interference of other legitimate uses of water bodies.

2. RECOGNITION OF THE IMPORT OF TECHNOLOGY AND OTHER ECONOMIC FACTORS IN ENVIRONMENTAL MANAGEMENT.

The declaration highlights the significance of technological and financial transfer as critical forms of assistance that enhance the remedying of environmental insufficiencies caused by under-

---

[91] Stockholm Convention on Persistent Organic Pollutants. "Principles 2 and 5." UNEP, www.pops.int/.".

[92] Stockholm Convention on Persistent Organic Pollutants. "Principles 3" UNEP, www.pops.int/."

[93] Stockholm Convention on Persistent Organic Pollutants. "Principles 4." UNEP, www.pops.int/."

development and natural disasters,[94] other economic factors such as the stability and fair pricing of commodities and raw materials also facilitate the management of the environment for developing countries.[95] In this regard, governments shoulder the obligation of formulating environmental policies that enhance the future development potential of their countries. Proper planning should enable the prohibition of the implementation of arcane policies that impede the realization of better living conditions for citizens.[96]

3. THE EMPHASIS ON THE ROLE OF THE INTERNATIONAL COMMUNITY IN ENVIRONMENTAL MANAGEMENT.

The international community should avail resources in form of technical assistance and financial assistance to developing countries in appropriate circumstances that require such countries to take certain steps to improve or preserve the environment. [97] States should integrate and coordinate their perceptions towards planning and development to accomplish rational management of resources to improve the environment, such an approach is important towards enhancing the compatibility of development with the population needs.[98]

4. THE EMPHASIS ON THE SIGNIFICANCE OF ENVIRONMENTAL PLANNING ON SUSTAINABLE DEVELOPMENT.

The declaration highlights the significance of balanced planning as an indispensable instrument in the reconciliation of conflicts between human needs, development, and environmental conservation.[99] Environmental planning is a critical aspect in human settlements and urbanization, for the avoidance of deleterious impacts upon the human environment as well as for utmost ecological and socio-economic advantages for all citizens.

---

[94] Stockholm Convention on Persistent Organic Pollutants. "Principles 9." UNEP, www.pops.int/."

[95] Stockholm Convention on Persistent Organic Pollutants. "Principles 10." UNEP, www.pops.int/."

[96] Stockholm Convention on Persistent Organic Pollutants. "Principles 11." UNEP, www.pops.int/."

[97] Stockholm Convention on Persistent Organic Pollutants. "Principles 12." UNEP, www.pops.int/."

[98] Stockholm Convention on Persistent Organic Pollutants. "Principles 13." UNEP, www.pops.int/."

[99] Stockholm Convention on Persistent Organic Pollutants. "Principles 14." UNEP, www.pops.int/."

5. EMPHASIS ON THE FORMULATION OF HUMAN RIGHTS COMPLIANT ENVIRONMENTAL POLICIES.

The Stockholm declaration emphasizes the need to abandon projects that augment human rights non-compliant, discriminative racist and colonialist domination. [100] State governments must endear to formulate appropriate unprejudiced and human rights compliant policies specifically for implementation in places with extremely dense populations that are likely to have undesirable consequences on development and the human environment. [101]

6. RECOGNITION OF THE ROLE OF STATE AUTHORITIES AND INSTITUTIONS IN ENVIRONMENTAL MANAGEMENT.

The declaration emphasizes the important function appropriate state authorities and institutions occupy in managing the environment. State institutions mandated to manage environmental resources need to undertake the role of planning, managing, and regulating national ecological resources to enhance environmental quality.[102]

7. THE EMPHASIS IS ON THE NEED TO CREATE ENVIRONMENTAL AWARENESS FOR SUSTAINABLE ENVIRONMENTAL MANAGEMENT.

The declaration affirms the need to endorse environmental consciousness through civic education on environmental matters for all generations of society including young, old, and disadvantaged citizens. This is important in expanding rational behavior and perspectives by persons and societies in conserving and reinforcing environmental governance. The electronic and mass media should promote positive environmental governance by disseminating positive and educational information on environmental management. [103]

8. RECOGNITION OF THE ROLE OF SCIENCE IN ENVIRONMENTAL MANAGEMENT

The declaration emphasizes the need for states to acknowledge and exploit science and technology in the identification, circumvention, and mitigation of environmental hazards for collective advantage.[104] States are required to support scientific research and development nationally,

---

[100] Stockholm Convention on Persistent Organic Pollutants. "Principles 15." UNEP, www.pops.int/."

[101] Stockholm Convention on Persistent Organic Pollutants. "Principles 16." UNEP, www.pops.int/."

[102] Stockholm Convention on Persistent Organic Pollutants. "Principles 17." UNEP, www.pops.int/."

[103] Stockholm Convention on Persistent Organic Pollutants. "Principles 18." UNEP, www.pops.int/."

[104] Stockholm Convention on Persistent Organic Pollutants. "Principles 19." UNEP, www.pops.int/."

regionally, and internationally in the scope of environmental management particularly in underdeveloped countries. In the same regard, authorities must promote the unrestricted flow of current scientific data and statistics to empower the development of a solution to environmental challenges. The transfer of Ecological technologies to developing nations, under unrestricted conditions, that do not impose an unnecessary economic burden on those countries is critical in achieving environmental conservation.[105].

9. EMPHASIS ON THE PRINCIPLE OF SOVEREIGNTY IN ENVIRONMENTAL DECISIONS.

The declaration supports the principle of sovereignty in environmental decisions as provided in the United Nations Charter on the principles of international law that accord states the sovereignty rights and powers to utilize natural and environmental resources according to their laws and ecological guiding principles. There is also an obligation to responsibly make sure that all undertakings within national territories and jurisdictions don't have deleterious consequences upon the environment and the surrounding environment of other countries outside their territorial limits in jurisdictions of other countries.[106]

10. EMPHASIS ON THE ROLE OF INTERNATIONAL COOPERATION IN ENVIRONMENTAL MANAGEMENT.

The declaration emphasizes the need for cooperation amongst states for the progressive improvement of the subject of international law on compensation and liability for persons afflicted by the degradation of the environment as well as the deleterious consequences of environmental pollution and other forms of ecological hazards, that emanate from the activities within the jurisdiction of such nations but extending to countries and areas beyond their jurisdiction. [107]in furtherance of this principle, the declaration affirms the cognizance that International affairs in the conservation of the environment are essentially best handled through a cooperative approach by all nations by either multilateral and bilateral agreements or other means that are indispensable in the effective regulation, mitigation, inhibition, deterrence and elimination of deleterious ecological impacts, resultant from actions that occur but in consideration of the sovereign nature of states and accruing interests.[108]Countries should ensure that international organizations

---

[105] Stockholm Convention on Persistent Organic Pollutants. "Principles 20." UNEP, www.pops.int/."

[106] Stockholm Convention on Persistent Organic Pollutants. "Principles 21." UNEP, www.pops.int/."

[107] Stockholm Convention on Persistent Organic Pollutants. "Principles 22." UNEP, www.pops.int/."

[108] Stockholm Convention on Persistent Organic Pollutants. "Principles 24" UNEP, www.pops.int/."

contribute in coordinated, dynamic, and effective roles in the conservation and enhancement of the environment. [109]On the same note, they must endeavor to reach timely agreements through relevant international institutions to safeguard Man and his environment from the consequences of the manufacture, testing, use, and disposal of nuclear armament and other destructive weapons.[110]

2.08. THE IMPACT OF THE RIO DECLARATION ON ENVIRONMENTAL POLICY AND DEVELOPMENT.

In June 1992 the 'Rio Declaration' formally took place. The convention has been critical in reaffirming and furthering the goals set out in the Stockholm conference. It established equitable partnerships and emphasized the need for cooperation amongst states and the adherence to international instruments that seek to preserve and protect the environment worldwide. Principle 1 of the declaration acknowledges the central role of humans amidst the apprehensions concerning sustainable development and the prerogative to a productive and healthy lifestyle that promotes a harmonious relationship with nature. [111] The conference also highlighted the need to foster equitable progress that meets the socio-economic development and ecological needs of the present and future generations,[112] by promoting environmental management and conservation as essential aspects of the achievement of sustainable development.[113]

A.) STATE OBLIGATIONS UNDER THE CONVENTION.

1. State cooperation in eradicating poverty.

The declaration emphasizes the need for cooperative

efforts in addressing and eliminating poverty by checking the disparity amongst global citizens as pertains to the living standards of people for sustainable development.[114]This obligation prioritizes environmental management alongside the development needs of developing and underdeveloped countries.[115]Cooperation and good faith are

---

[109] Stockholm Convention on Persistent Organic Pollutants. "Principles 25." UNEP, www.pops.int/."

[110] Stockholm Convention on Persistent Organic Pollutants. "Principles 26." UNEP, www.pops.int/."

[111]United Nations. "The Rio Declaration on Environment and Development: Principle 1." United Nations Sustainable Development KnowledgePlatform,www.un.org/en/development/desa/population/migration/generalassembly/d ocs/global compact/A_CONF.151_26_Vol.I_Declaration.pdf.

[112] United Nations. "The Rio Declaration on Environment and Development: Principle 2." Ibid [113] United Nations. "The Rio Declaration on Environment and Development: Principle 4." Ibid [114] United Nations. "The Rio Declaration on Environment and Development: Principle 5." Ibid [115] United Nations. "The Rio Declaration on Environment and Development: Principle 6." Ibid

vital in fostering partnerships that fulfill the values of environmental management and the progress of international law in line with sustainable development.[116]

2. State efforts in enhancing environmental conservation.

States must cooperate to facilitate environmental conservation, protection, and the restoration of the earth's ecological ecosystems. Developing countries must promote sustainable development regarding the constant societal pressures emanating from technological and financial developments.[117]To attain improved standards of living for citizens as well as sustainable development. States have the obligation of reducing and eliminating unsustainable production and consumption patterns alongside promoting suitable demographic policies.[118] States are obliged to take necessary precautions as an approach toward protecting the environment. in circumstances where there is a possibility of irreversible and adverse consequences to the environment, where there exist threats of grave or irremediable harm, or where accurate scientific certainty is absent, there shouldn't be an excuse for scientific certainty as a reason for suspending appropriate cost- effective procedures to avert environmental dilapidation.[119]

3. Capacity Building and strengthening of scientific efforts.

States have an obligation of cooperating to strengthen capacity-building toward sustainable development. States should work towards fostering and improving scientific understanding by way of the exchange of scientific information and technology transfer to enhance innovative adaptation.[120]

4. Promoting Public Participation in Environmental affairs.

States must promote public participation in environmental issues at all levels, this obligation requires states to provide citizens with the relevant information to ensure they make informed choices. The information includes information on hazardous elements and activities in their societies.[121]

---

[116] United Nations. "The Rio Declaration on Environment and Development: Principle 27 Ibid [117] United Nations. "The Rio Declaration on Environment and Development: Principle 7

Ibid [118] United Nations. "The Rio Declaration on Environment and Development: Principle 8

Ibid [119] United Nations. "The Rio Declaration on Environment and Development: Principle 15

Ibid [120] United Nations. "The Rio Declaration on Environment and Development: Principle 9

Ibid [121] United Nations. "The Rio Declaration on Environment and Development: Principle 10 Ibid

5. Enacting effective environmental legislation.

States should enact effective legislation on environmental management standards with relevant priorities that reflect appropriate environmental contexts upon which they apply. Applicable standards should not burden other states or societies through unnecessary economic and social.[122]

6. Promoting growth and development through sustainable economic systems.

States have an obligation of cooperating and promoting open economic systems that foster socio-economic growth and progress for sustainability in development. This is critical for all states to effectively address challenges that affect the environment such as environmental degradation. Policies should not constitute discriminatory, arbitrary, and unjustified restrictions that stifle international trade. All international measures aimed at dealing with transboundary environmental issues should involve international consensus.[123]

7. Developing guidelines on liability and compensation of victims of environmental effects. States should develop national legislation and guidelines regarding polluters' liability as well as a recompensing for victims of environmental hazards or pollution. This obligation extends to the prompt cooperation amongst states for the growth of international law as pertains to the liability of parties and compensation of victims for the adverse consequences of actions leading to environmental degradation within their national jurisdiction and beyond.[124]

8. Discouraging the transfer of hazardous substances across borders.

States should cooperate in discouraging the movement and transfer of hazardous substances that have deleterious environmental implications or consequential damage to the environment as well as the health of people in those other states.[125]

9. Internalization of economic measures

National authorities have an obligation of promoting the internalization of economic measures including the polluter pay principle in consideration of public interest and without any economic interruption or restrictions to international trade.[126]

---

[122] United Nations. "The Rio Declaration on Environment and Development: Principle 11 Ibid [123]United Nations. "The Rio Declaration on Environment and Development: Principle 12 Ibid [124]United Nations. "The Rio Declaration on Environment and Development: Principle 13 Ibid [125] United Nations. "The Rio Declaration on Environment and Development: Principle 14 Ibid [126]United Nations. "The Rio Declaration on Environment and Development: Principle 16 Ibid

10. Carrying out Environmental Impact assessment.

States have an obligation of embodying the principles of environmental impact assessment as a mandatory nationwide tool essential before the commencement of any projects and activities to mitigate adverse effects upon the environment.[127]

11. Duty of the state in providing information.

States have an obligation of providing information to other parties. States must inform their counterparts across borders of imminent natural catastrophes and disasters bound to inflict adverse impacts on the environment or ecological heritage of those nations. This obligation extends to international assistance to afflicted states.[128] States should expeditiously provide appropriate information in good faith to states in the danger of being negatively affected through transboundary activities.[129]

12. Recognizing the role of special interest groups in environmental management.

States have an obligation towards recognizing the role of women in sustainable development as a critical aspect of the achievement and accomplishment of sustainable development.[130]The courage borne by the youthful populations and their creativity globally must be organized to foster constructive partnerships in the accomplishment of sustainable development for all human beings.[131]States must also recognize the role of indigenous societies and their people in environmental conservation and development since these societies possess special knowledge and traditional practices by supporting the identity, cultural heritage, and special interests of these societies to facilitate efficient participation in the accomplishment of the sustainable development goals.[132] This obligation also includes the responsibility of preserving, respecting, and protecting the environment and ecological resources of any people under domination or oppression.[133]

13. State obligation in upholding international law.

States are obliged to uphold international law as regards environmental management and conservation even in times of warfare and armed conflict.[134] Parties must recognize that peace and

---

[127] United Nations. "The Rio Declaration on Environment and Development: Principle 17 Ibid [128] United Nations. "The Rio Declaration on Environment and Development: Principle 18 Ibid [129] United Nations. "The Rio Declaration on Environment and Development: Principle 19 Ibid [130] United Nations. "The Rio Declaration on Environment and Development: Principle 20 Ibid [131] United Nations. "The Rio Declaration on Environment and Development: Principle 21 Ibid [132] United Nations. "The Rio Declaration on Environment and Development: Principle 22 Ibid [133] United Nations. "The Rio Declaration on Environment and Development: Principle 23 Ibid [134] United Nations. "The Rio Declaration on Environment and Development: Principle 24 Ibid

development go hand in hand with environmental protection,[135] and that it is imperative to have all environmental disputes resolved through peaceful channels and by suitable means as stipulated in the United Nations Charter.[136]

2.09.POST MODERN ERA.

The state has emerged as a central and critical form of political organization in One of the most significant developments in world history. According to the guidelines of international law by which people strive to create a state I.e. the control of a definite territory, possession of an effective form of government as well as the ability to interact with other sovereign states.[137] In the Post- modern Era, however, the International law on the environment encounters a significantly evolving globe exemplified by increasing movements of political power that exists outside the confines of traditional governmental structures in regional, global and international organizations as well as in a transnational corporation.[138]Post the Stockholm conference, the debate on the legislation of environmental law has progressively taken shape subject to discourse across the world, the subject draws attention from state bodies, economic organizations, and legal scholars.

There are diverse issues that manifest in the subject of environmental law from a global perspective including those that touch on fundamental legal principles associated with individual rights, the right of nations to determine their affairs (sovereignty), the management of shared resources, collective efforts towards reducing the global carbon footprint, sustainable energy consumption patterns as well as reforms in economic development and an appreciation of the effects of human activity in the environment in the post-modern era. The discussions around these issues have led to the negotiation of various multilateral agreements over the years, at various levels internationally. Some agreements have limited Parties while others have a vast international membership.[139]In the Post-Modern Era in the international arena, perspectives on the subject of environmental law have evolved through intellectual discourse from a niche of environmental and legal scholars, through the ratification of international agreements, international conventions, and

[135]United Nations. "The Rio Declaration on Environment and Development: Principle 25 Ibid [136] United Nations. "The Rio Declaration on Environment and Development: Principle 24 Ibid [137] Koivurova, Timo. *Introduction to International Environmental Law*. Routledge, Taylor & Francis, Page 2, para. 2.

[138] Koivurova, Timo. *Introduction to International Environmental Law*. Routledge, Taylor & Francis, Page 1 Para 3.

[139] International Environmental Law Multilateral Environmental Agreements. Page 12, para. 4. Available at. http://www.oas.org/dsd/tool- kit/ Documentos/MOduleII/Multilateral %20Environmental%20Agreements.pdf

regional treatises that augment the evolution of international environmental law. The outcome of mutual environmental agreements forms a part of the international conventions recognized by the Statute of the International Court of Justice in Article 38 (1) as a source of international law on the subject of environmental affairs.[140]

2.10. The Outcome and Influence of Mutual Environmental Agreements in International Environmental Law

1. Comprehensive Legislation and Regulation

Modern environmental laws are redefining environmental governance by introducing comprehensive legislation and regulations that cover a wide array of environmental issues. These laws address not only pollution control but also conservation, biodiversity, climate change, and sustainable development. By consolidating diverse aspects of environmental management under a unified legal framework, governments can more effectively oversee environmental protection efforts.

2.INTERNATIONAL COOPERATION AND AGREEMENTS

Environmental laws today emphasize international cooperation through treaties and agreements. Global challenges such as climate change and transboundary pollution require collaborative efforts between nations. Agreements like the Paris Agreement on climate change and conventions like the Basel Convention on the Control of Transboundary Movements of Hazardous Wastes and Their Disposal promote shared responsibilities and common standards, ensuring a unified approach to environmental governance on a global scale.

3.INCORPORATING INDIGENOUS KNOWLEDGE AND COMMUNITY INVOLVEMENT

Modern environmental laws are recognizing the importance of traditional ecological knowledge held by indigenous communities. These laws promote the active involvement of local communities in environmental decision-making processes. By integrating indigenous wisdom and local perspectives, environmental governance becomes more inclusive, ensuring that policies are culturally sensitive and sustainable in the long term.

4.ADAPTABILITY AND FLEXIBILITY

Contemporary environmental laws are designed to be adaptable and flexible to accommodate rapid scientific advancements and changing environmental challenges. Provisions are included to revise regulations based on new scientific findings, emerging technologies, and evolving environmental

---

[140] Ibidem

threats. This adaptability ensures that environmental governance remains relevant and effective in addressing emerging issues such as plastic pollution, emerging contaminants, and novel biodiversity threats.

5. PROMOTING CORPORATE SOCIAL RESPONSIBILITY AND ACCOUNTABILITY

Modern environmental laws hold corporations accountable for their environmental impact. Through stringent regulations, corporate social responsibility initiatives, and penalties for non-compliance, these laws encourage businesses to adopt sustainable practices. By fostering a sense of environmental responsibility among corporations, environmental governance becomes more robust, leading to reduced pollution, efficient resource management, and overall ecological sustainability.

2.11. The status of Compliance and Implementation of Environmental Law under Kenyan Law.

Kenya is a member of the Convention on Biological Diversity (CBD), an outcome of the United Nations Conference on Environment and Development held in Rio de Janeiro in 1992. Kenya is also keen on implementing other international development treaties like Agenda 21 and the Millennium Development Goals that are inclined to environment protection and sustainable development.[141] Environmental governance in Kenya is based on a set of principles that are provided for in the Kenyan Constitution of 2010 which is the supreme law of the Republic and other regulations which form Acts of parliament. The relevant provisions of the constitution concerning environmental governance are supported by the Acts of parliament and enforced by various authorities provided for in the Acts besides other judicial institutions and special Quasi- judicial institutions. The subject of environmental jurisprudence and governance in Kenya was less regarded and explored in the last decades before the promulgation of the Constitution of Kenya in 2010; this was partly because of the unpopularity and lack of expertise in environmental law. In the last decade, however, environmental law has progressively developed and gained impetus whilst environmental consciousness amongst many citizens has greatly taken shape. The promulgation of the Kenyan constitution of 2010 was therefore a historic milestone in Kenya's Environmental governance, policy development, and implementation. Kenya has also put in place

---

[141]sustainable Development in Kenya: Stocktaking in the Run up to Rio+20." United Nations Department of Economic and Social Affairs, 2012, https://sustainabledevelopment.un.org/content/documents/985kenya.pdf.

a wide range of policy, institutional and legislative frameworks to address the major causes of environmental degradation and negative impacts on ecosystems emanating from industrial and economic development programs. The Environmental Management and Coordination Act of 1999 (EMCA) provides the requisite legal and institutional framework for the management of the environment.

2.12. The significance of the Constitution of Kenya 2010 on Environmental Governance.
a.) Recognition of international law as an integral part of Kenyan law.
- **Article 2 (5) of the constitution of Kenya 2010**

National integration and cooperation in environmental governance have progressively grown out of national concerns and acknowledgment of the collective burden on environmental degradation in Kenya, as well as the need to tackle environmental challenges posed by development and globalization among other factors. International conventions and treaties have immensely contributed to the national framework of Environmental regulations and environmental standards in Kenya. Article 2 (5) of the constitution of Kenya 2010 recognizes international law as an integral part of Kenyan law, the constitution acknowledges the general rules of international law as part of the law in the Republic of Kenya.[142] Article 2 (6) also provides that any treaty or convention ratified by Kenya is recognized as part of the law of Kenya under the Constitution.[143]

B.) THE EMPHASIS ON THE ROLE OF PUBLIC PARTICIPATION IN ENVIRONMENTAL MANAGEMENT

- **Article 10 of the Constitution of Kenya 2010.**

Article 10 of The Constitution of Kenya 2010 recognizes the significance of public participation in environmental conservation and governance. The National values and principles of governance bind state organs in the application and interpretation of the constitution, in the enactment of laws, and in the implementation of decisions that have implications on the public such as public policy decisions. This provision requires state organs to facilitate and implement public participation in environmental governance and to promote sustainable development or development that meets the needs of the present without compromising the needs of future generations.[144]

c.) The emphasis on the role of Sustainable Development in Environmental management

- **Article 10 of the Constitution of Kenya 2010.**

Sustainable development as provided for in the Kenyan constitution of 2010 implies the kind and type of socio-economic progress that attains the requirements of the current generations devoid of compromising the needs of prospective generations.[145] Article 10 of The Constitution of Kenya 2010 recognizes the importance of public sustainable development in the conservation of

---

[142] Constitution of Kenya 2010, Article 2(5).

[143] Constitution of Kenya 2010, Article 2(6).

[144] Constitution of Kenya 2010 Article 10.

[145] Constitution of Kenya 2010, Article 10.

management of the environment. Article 10 places an obligation upon state organs to facilitate and promote sustainable development.

d.) Concerning the Protection of Indigenous seeds and plant varieties.

- **Article 11 of the Constitution of Kenya 2010.**

Article 11 of the Constitution of Kenya 2010 places the obligation upon the legislative arms of government to legislate and enact legislation that recognizes and protects the ownership of plant varieties, indigenous seeds, their genetic and diverse characteristics as well as their utilization and exploitation by Kenyan communities.[146] The state is obliged to care for genetic resources and biological diversity from destruction and degradation through the establishment of guidelines and systems regarding environmental impact assessment activity and mitigating mechanisms, alongside other environmental management structures such as environmental monitoring and audit. Such systems are critical in the effective management of the environment and the efficient utilization of the environment and its natural resources for the profit of the people of Kenya.[147]

a.) Entitlement to the Right to a Clean and Healthy Environment.

- **Article 42 of the Constitution of Kenya 2010.**

The constitution is the supreme law in Kenya.[148] It provides for the right to a clean and healthy environment [149] that entitles citizens the right to a clean and healthy environment and emphasizes the duty to safeguard and enhance the environment. Article 42 further affirms every person's right to have the environment protected by way of legislative measures to benefit the present and future generations. [150]

B.) OBLIGATIONS CONCERNING THE ENVIRONMENT.

- **Article 69 of the Constitution of Kenya 2010.**

This provision obliges the state and state entities to ensure sustainable utilization, exploitation, conservation, and management of environmental and resources to facilitate fair distribution of accruing environmental benefits. The state is required to take the necessary measures to fulfill the obligations provided for above including working towards the achievement and maintenance of a least ten percent tree cover of the territory of Kenya, ensuring that the intellectual property

[146] Constitution of Kenya 2010, Article 11(3).

[147] Constitution of Kenya 2010, Article 69.

[148] Constitution of Kenya 2010, Article 2 (5).

regarding traditional knowledge on biodiversity as well as the communities' genetic resources are enhanced and protected by encouraging members of the public to participate in the protection, management, and conservation of the environment.

C.) THE ENFORCEMENT OF ENVIRONMENTAL RIGHTS.

- **Article 70 of the Constitution of Kenya 2010.**

This section of the constitution contains provisions that contain statutory remedies in cases where the environment is being degraded. Where a person asserts that environmental rights are being or will be infringed, violated, or denied the person is at liberty to approach a court to seek rectification of such circumstances and to have the right protected besides other available legal remedies. The courts have the authority to issue appropriate orders to discontinue and to prevent any actions or omissions that are deleterious or that negatively alter the environment. The courts may also compel a public officer to take administrative and legal actions to avert or suspend harmful acts or to provide liability and compensation to victims of environmental hazards and degradation.[151]

D.) PRINCIPLES OF LAND USE

- **Article 64 of the Constitution of Kenya 2010.**

The constitution of Kenya 2010 provides guidelines regarding land tenure and most importantly land use. The Law requires that land be utilized optimally and in the best sustainable way. The principles of sustainability and equity apply in the utilization of land resources.

2.13. The Institutional Framework of Kenya's Environmental governance.

a.) The Role of the Land and Environmental courts in Environmental management.

The land and environmental courts have the Jurisdiction and status of High courts in Kenya but are essentially specialized courts that only deal with environmental and Land issues. The constitution of Kenya 2010 has created the special courts with the status and authority of the High court to hear and determine matters relating to land and the environment. The entire Fifth Chapter of the Kenyan constitution of 2010 is dedicated to equitable principles of Land as a natural resource and matters about the Environment. The Chapter provides the foundation for the law on land and the basic principles that govern Land and the environment.[152]

---

[151]Constitution of Kenya 2010, Article 70.

[152]Constitution of Kenya 2010, Chapter 5.

b.) The National Environmental Management Authority.

The National Environment Management Authority is a statutory body formed under the Environmental Management and Coordination Act. It is the primary regulatory body under the Ministry of Environment and Mineral Resources in Kenya. The authority is responsible for environmental coordination in Kenya.

c.) The Ministry of Agriculture and the ministry of public health and sanitation.

The Ministry of public health and sanitation and its agencies are involved in the coordination and regulation of matters concerning Public Health, such as the management of hazardous wastes and radiation control as well as the management of water resources and utilization through the and the Ministry of water development. The Ministry of Agriculture as well Controls farming practices to prevent soil erosion in areas with sloppy land.[153]

2.14. Functions of the National Environmental Management Authority.

i. **Advisory Role** - The National Environmental Management Authority advises the Kenyan Government concerning important and consequential international and regional environmental accords such as international conventions, agreements, and treaties as pertains to environmental governance environmental. The Authority further recommends to the Kenyan government the conventions and treaties that Kenya should be a party to, follows up pursues, and implement agreements.

ii. **Coordination of Research and Investigation** -The National Environmental Management Authority

Co-ordinates the environmental management activities carried out by various authorities such as lead agencies and promotes the incorporation of ecological concerns into development guidelines, strategies, and Programmes to ensure appropriate Management and coherent exploitation of environmental resources on the betterment of the human life in Kenya.[154] Authority coordinates investigations and undertakes research, conducts environmental surveys, collects, collates, and disseminates scientific findings from such research and investigation.

iii. **Mobilization of Resources** -The Authority is tasked with the mobilization and monitoring of resources such as financial and human resources in Environmental management.

---

[153] sustainable Development in Kenya: Stocktaking in the Run up to Rio+20." United Nations Department of Economic and Social Affairs, 2012, https://sustainabledevelopment.un.org/content/documents/985kenya.pdf.

[154] Environmental Management and Coordination Act. Section 3.

iv. **Identification of Programmes and Projects -** The National Environmental Management Authority identifies projects that require environmental management, audit monitoring, and environmental impact assessment.

v. **Initiation of safety Procedures -** National Environmental Management Authority initiates and evolves procedures and safeguards for the prevention of accidents that may cause environmental degradation. The authority also evolves corrective procedures where accidents take place.

vi. **Monitoring and assessment -**National Environmental Management Authority Is involved in the monitoring and assessment of various activities to make certain that t such activities do not degrade the environment. This is important in the achievement of ecological management goals as well as early communication to the public on impending environmental disasters

vii. **Cooperation and sharing of information with lead agencies -**The National Environmental Management Authority cooperate with relevant institutions and agencies in the implementation of programs anticipated to improve public consciousness and environmental education. These programs are critical in enhancing sound environmental administration as and encourage the effort of other active environmental action groups.

viii. **Publication and dissemination of manuals -** The National Environmental Management Authority publishes and disseminates information about environmental management through manuals, newsletters, and guidelines that contribute to environmental education and awareness as well as the prevention of environmental degradation.

ix. **Technical Support -**The National Environmental Management Authority renders advice and technical support, to institutions and persons that are involved in the conservation and management of environmental resources.

x. **Annual Reporting** –The National Environmental Management Authority prepares and issues an annual report on the state of the environment in Kenya and may direct any lead agency to prepare and submit to it a report on the state of the sector of the Environment under the administration of that lead agency.

xi. **Taking stock of the natural resources** - The National Environmental Management Authority also conducts stock-taking of the existing environmental resources and monitors the utilization of the natural resources. The authority further reviews and establishes guidelines regarding the utilization of land as well as the impacts of such activities on the quality and quantity of natural resources.

xii.   **Carrying out Surveys-** The National Environmental Management Authority facilitates surveys that promote proper Conservation and management of the environment. The Authority also advises the Government on legislative measures for the Management of the environment and the implementation of appropriate, treaties, international conventions, and agreements in Environmental management.

D.)THE COMPLAINTS COMMITTEE

The Complaints Committee investigates any complaints and allegations against a person or Authority as pertains to the state of the environment in Kenya. The Complaints Committee investigates allegations on its motion regarding cases of environmental contamination and Degradation, the committee makes a report of its findings and recommendations to the Council.

E.) THE ENVIRONMENTAL INSPECTORS.

The Office of Environmental inspectors is an authority under the Environmental Management and Coordination Act; inspectors enforce the provisions of the Act through innumerable procedures. The Act, therefore, accords them diverse powers to enforce and monitor compliance with the various provisions of the Act. An environmental inspector is authorized in the performance of his duties under the Act or other relevant environmental regulations to enter any land at any times premises, or vessels without a warrant, to make examinations and inquiries to determine whether the provisions of the Environmental Management and Coordination Act are complied with.

2.15. FUNCTIONS OF THE ENVIRONMENTAL INSPECTORS.

1. **Monitoring compliance with environmental standards** – Environmental inspectors are tasked with the responsibility of monitoring compliance with the environmental standards under the Environmental Management and coordination Act as well as the activities of other sector-specific environmental inspectorates. They also monitor the pattern of use of environmental resources.

2. **Conducting environmental audits-** Environmental inspectors conduct environmental audits. During the process they are authorized and required to inspect, and examine copies of licenses and may require the persons or entities involved to produce copies of the prerequisite approval documents including, Registers, records, and other documents relating to the environment and the management of natural resources;

3. **Collection of Samples-** Environmental Inspectors are authorized to collect and submit samples of any articles and substances to which any analysis may be required to ascertain contamination or pollution standards.

4.   **Inspection of Premises-** Environmental inspectors are authorized and required to carry out periodic inspections of all establishments and undertakings within their respective jurisdictional limits which manufacture, produce as by-products, import, export, store, sell, distribute or use any substances that are likely to have a significant impact on the environment, to ensure that the prescribed environmental standards according to the environmental regulations of the Environmental Management and Coordination Act and other laws are complied with.

Powers of Environmental inspectors.

1.   **Power of seizure and confiscation** - The environmental inspectors are authorized under the Act to confiscate any vessel, article, plant, equipment motor vehicle, or material that has been used in the commission of an offense under the environmental management and coordination Act.

2.   **Power to close any manufacturing plant-** The environmental inspectors are authorized to order the closure and seizure of the operation of any undertaking such as a manufacturing plant or other establishment which pollutes or is likely to contaminate the environment in contravention of environmental guidelines and regulations under the Environmental Management and Coordination Act or other environmental regulations in force.

3.   **Power to direct and require the implementation of remedial measures-** In furtherance of Kenya's guiding principles of Environmental conservation as provided under the Constitution of Kenya 2010 as well as the Environmental Management and coordination Act and other environmental legislation, the inspectors are authorized to direct

occupiers of undertakings or operators of polluting such establishment to put into place corrective procedures to prevent adverse or harmful effects to the environment.

4. **Powers to order and person to stop polluting the environment**- The Environmental inspectors have the mandate to issue improvement notices that require any persons operating polluting undertakings such as vessels, manufacturing plants, motor vehicles, and any polluting plants to discontinue any actions that are harmful to the environment. Environmental inspectors may also take suitable corrective measures that include facilitating the putting in place of appropriate alternative plants and machinery within a reasonable time as may be determined by the director-general.

2.17. Kenya's National Environment Action Plan

Kenya's Environment Action plan contains an analysis of the natural resources of Kenya with an Indication as to patterns of change in their distribution and Quantity over time as well as an analytical profile of the various uses and value of the Natural resources incorporating considerations of intergenerational Equity. The Action plan also recommends appropriate legal and fiscal incentives that encourage stakeholders to incorporate environmental Requirements into their planning and operational processes.

- **NATIONAL ENVIRONMENTAL AWARENESS**

Kenya's Environmental Action Plan Identifies and recommends policy and legislative approaches for regulating and mitigating adverse impacts of human activity on the environment by facilitating the prioritization of research in environmental Management. The plan recommends techniques that promote national awareness of Environmental education and the utility of sustainable exploitation of Environmental resources for human development. These techniques are significant as operational guidelines in the management of environmental resources as they facilitate the identification of real or perceived challenges that affect the environment as well as natural resources.

Environmental awareness is important in the identification and appraisal of urban development plans and rural settlements and the consequences of these developments on the environment. It promotes strategies for the mitigation of the deleterious consequences of development as well as the proposal of regulations for the integration of environmental conservation standards in development planning and management.

- **Gas flaring and venting regulations in Kenya.**

Kenya's Environmental Management and Coordination Act provide various provisions for the regulation of noxious smells. The National Environmental and Management Authority is required in consultation with appropriate agencies to institute measures and mechanisms to measure and determine the levels of poisonous smells and the minimum standards essential in regulating environmental degradation emanating from toxic smells. These minimum regulations are expected to contain measures capable of abating deleterious emissions from human activities and naturally existing phenomena.[155]

---

[155] Environmental Management and Coordination Act, Section 107. [155]

2.18. The Impact of International Environmental Law On Kenya's Legislative Framework and Environmental Governance.

The international development of environmental law has significantly shaped Kenya's legislative framework on environmental governance. Over the years, international environmental agreements and conventions, such as the Stockholm Convention on Persistent Organic Pollutants and the Paris Agreement on climate change, have played a pivotal role in guiding global efforts toward sustainable environmental practices. These international instruments have influenced Kenya's policies, leading to the enactment of various laws and regulations aimed at protecting the environment. Kenya, like many other nations, has realized the importance of aligning its domestic legislation with international standards to address transboundary environmental issues effectively. Consequently, the country has incorporated principles from these global agreements into its legal system, fostering the development of robust environmental governance mechanisms. This integration not only demonstrates Kenya's commitment to global environmental preservation but also ensures that the nation is in harmony with the international community, fostering collaboration and shared responsibility in addressing environmental challenges. In Kenya, the impact of international environmental law on the legislative framework is evident in the formulation and implementation of laws promoting sustainable development and environmental conservation. The country has actively participated in international environmental agreements, which has influenced the enactment of laws addressing issues such as pollution control, biodiversity conservation, and climate change mitigation. Kenya's legislative response reflects its commitment to meeting international standards and fulfilling its obligations under various environmental treaties. Moreover, the alignment of Kenya's environmental laws with international agreements has led to the establishment of regulatory bodies, enforcement mechanisms, and monitoring systems to ensure compliance and accountability. By incorporating international principles, Kenya has strengthened its environmental governance, paving the way for a more sustainable future and contributing to the global efforts to safeguard the planet for generations to come.

CHAPTER 3

NAVIGATING THE PATH OF SUSTAINABLE DEVELOPMENT IN THE FACE OF CLIMATE CHANGE" A GLIMPSE INTO THE PAST, PRESENT, AND FUTURE

3.01. INTRODUCTION TO SUSTAINABLE DEVELOPMENT

The concept of Sustainable Development was coined at the United Nations Conference on the Human Environment in Stockholm in 1972 and subsequently defined through the World Conservation Strategy (1980), the Brundtland Report (1987), and the United Nations Conference on Environment and Development in Rio (1992)[156]. Sustainable development refers to development that meets the needs of the present generation without compromising the ability of future generations to meet their needs by maintaining the carrying capacity of the supporting ecosystems.[157] Sustainable development emphasizes the preservation of natural resources, biodiversity, and ecosystems, ensuring a balanced relationship between human activities and the environment. The concept therefore fundamentally obligates the state as well as its citizens to prudently manage, exploit and utilize its natural resources from the environment to ensure optimum realization of planned economic and social goals in the present as well as future generations. By promoting sustainable economic practices, countries can achieve long-term economic stability, reducing the risks associated with resource depletion and environmental degradation.[158]

Sustainable development transcends national boundaries and has henceforth become a global priority. The essence of Sustainable Development lies in the principle of "meeting the needs of the present without compromising the ability of future generations to meet their own needs.[159] Sustainable development focuses on social equity, ensuring that economic progress benefits all, to grasp the concept of sustainability, one must consider the three fundamental areas of influence, commonly referred to as the "Three Pillars of Sustainability": Social, Economic, and Environmental aspects. These aspects are intricately interconnected, and when integrated and applied in real-world scenarios,

---

[156] Introduction to Sustainable Development: A Brief Handbook for Students by Students. International Hellenic University, 2015.

[157] Ibidem

[158] Pearce, D., & Barbier, E. B. (2000). Blueprint for a sustainable economy. Earthscan Publications.

159 United Nations General Assembly, 1987, p. 43

160 Sen, A. (1999). Development as Freedom. Oxford University Press.

they can establish a stable foundation for a sustainable world that benefits everyone. In such a framework, natural resources are conserved, the environment is safeguarded, the economy remains unharmed, and the quality of life for people is either enhanced or preserved.[161]

3.02. Historical Background and Evolution of Sustainable Development Concepts The historical background and evolution of sustainable development concepts trace a transformative journey in environmental conservation, social equity, and economic progress. Rooted in early environmental movements, the concept of sustainable development gained prominence during the latter half of the 20th century.

a.) The Rise of Awareness of Environmental Issues -"*Silent Spring,*"

The 1960s and 1970s witnessed a growing awareness of environmental issues, sparked by events like the publication of Rachel Carson's influential book "Silent Spring," which highlighted the detrimental effects of pesticides on the environment. This awareness led to the first Earth Day in 1970, uniting people in their concerns about environmental degradation.[162] Upon Carson's death just eighteen months later in the spring of 1964, at the age of fifty-six, she had initiated a series of events that eventually led to the domestic production ban of DDT in the United States and the emergence of a grassroots movement advocating for environmental protection through state and federal regulations. Carson's literary work sparked a profound shift in the way humans perceived and interacted with the natural world, triggering a heightened awareness of environmental issues within the public consciousness

b) The Brundtland Report of 1987- *Our Common Future*

The 1980s marked a significant turning point with the release of the Brundtland Report in 1987. Published by the United Nations World Commission on Environment and Development, the report defined sustainable development as "development that meets the needs of the present without compromising the ability of future generations to meet their own needs." This definition emphasized the interconnectedness of environmental, social, and economic factors, laying the foundation for the modern understanding of sustainable development. In the 1990s and early 2000s, sustainable development became a global priority. [163] Examining the evolution from Agenda 21, an action plan established at the Earth Summit in 1992, to the Sustainable

---

[161] Ibidem

[162] Carson, Rachel. *Silent Spring*. First Mariner Books edition, Houghton Mifflin Harcourt, 2002.

[163] World Commission on Environment and Development. *Our Common Future*. Oxford University Press, 1987.

Development Goals (SDGs) in 2015 provides insights into the international commitment to address pressing issues such as poverty, inequality, climate change, and environmental degradation.

3.03. The October 1984 and April 1987 series of devastating global events.

- **A million Deaths as a result of Drought in Africa**

In the span of 900 days between October 1984 and April 1987, the World Commission on Environment and Development bore witness to a series of devastating global events. During this period, Africa grappled with a severe crisis triggered by drought, endangering 36 million people and claiming the lives of possibly a million individuals.

• UNION CARBIDE CHEMICAL PLANT EXPLOSION IN BHOPAL INDIA

In Bhopal, India, a leak from a pesticides factory resulted in the tragic deaths of over 2,000 people while leaving more than 200,000 others injured or blinded.[164] The explosion that occurred in 1984 at the Union Carbide chemical plant in Bhopal, India, stands as an unquestionable epitome of one of the world's most devastating industrial disasters. Opinions about its repercussions diverge widely. Some assert that the ensuing legal battles established an "innovative model" for addressing the worldwide dispersion of technological risks. For others, the disaster marked a pivotal moment in the evolution of environmental legislation, reshaping the way nations approached industrial safety and corporate accountability. Yet, there are those who contend that Bhopal epitomizes the tangible, real-world manifestation of globalization, illustrating the complex and far-reaching impacts of global interconnectedness on local communities and the environment.[165]

•CATASTROPHIC EXPLOSION OF LIQUID GAS TANKS AT MEXICO CITY

At the same time Mexico City experienced a catastrophic explosion of liquid gas tanks, leading to the loss of 1,000 lives and rendering thousands homeless. On November 19, 1984, Mexico faced its most devastating industrial disaster when a liquid petroleum gas (LPG) plant was completely obliterated in a series of explosions. The tragic incident led to the loss of over 500 lives, left approximately 2,500 individuals injured, and resulted in the near-complete destruction of a seven- block area in a working-class neighborhood adjacent to the facility. It became evident within hours that the explosions had originated within the storage plant itself, which was owned and operated by PEMEX, the national oil corporation. While official confirmation of PEMEX's responsibility

---

[164] Fortun, Kim. *Advocacy after Bhopal: Environmentalism, Disaster, New Global Orders.* University of Chicago Press, 2001.

[165] Ibidem

took several weeks, questions were raised promptly about the corporation's safety record and its judgment in siting the plant within a densely populated urban area.

The public outcry and mounting criticism swiftly placed both the government and PEMEX, its influential state-owned enterprise, in a defensive position. After addressing the immediate challenges of rescue operations and emergency assistance, the government shifted its focus to mitigating the political fallout resulting from the catastrophe.[166]

Meanwhile, Europe faced the aftermath of the Chernobyl nuclear reactor explosion, as nuclear fallout spread across the continent, heightening the risks of future human cancers. On April 26, 1986, the Chernobyl nuclear power plant, located 100 km north of Kiev in Ukraine, experienced the most devastating incident in the history of the nuclear industry. The accident, which occurred in Unit 4 of the plant, resulted in a ten-day-long reactor fire, leading to an unparalleled release of radioactive material that contaminated over 200,000 km2 of European territory, particularly affecting areas in Belarus, the Russian Federation, and Ukraine. The aftermath of the disaster brought about immediate and long-term adverse effects on both the public and the environment. It also had profound psycho-social and economic repercussions on the affected populations and cast a shadow over the global nuclear industry. In response to the catastrophe, the international community swiftly engaged in assessments and practical efforts to mitigate the consequences of the Chernobyl accident. The IAEA played a pivotal role by organizing the first post-accident review meeting in August 1986. At the request of the Soviet Government in 1990, the IAEA coordinated a comprehensive assessment of the radiological consequences and evaluated protective measures. These initiatives marked the beginning of international collaboration aimed at understanding and mitigating the far-reaching impacts of the Chernobyl disaster.[167]

166 Johnson, Kirsten, "State and community during the aftermath of Mexico City's November 19, 1984 Gas Explosion" (1985). FMHI Publications. 58. https://digitalcommons.Usf.edu/fmhI pub/58 167 International Conference on Chernobyl: Looking Back to go Forward (2005: Vienna, Austria). *Proceedings of an International Conference on Chernobyl: Looking Back to Go Forward*, organized by the International Atomic Energy Agency on behalf of the Chernobyl Forum and held in Vienna, 6–7 September 2005.

•CHEMICALS, SOLVENTS, AND MERCURY FLOW INTO THE RHINE RIVER

Environmental disasters continued to unfold when a warehouse fire in Switzerland caused agricultural chemicals, solvents, and mercury to flow into the Rhine River. This event resulted in the deaths of millions of fish and posed a significant threat to the drinking water supplies in the Federal Republic of Germany and the Netherlands. Tragically, during this period, an estimated 60 million people succumbed to diarrheal diseases, a consequence of unsafe drinking water and malnutrition. Most heartbreaking was the fact that the majority of these victims were children, highlighting the urgent need for comprehensive global environmental policies and sustainable practices to prevent such devastating losses in the future.[168]

3.04. THE UNITED NATIONS EARTH SUMMIT HELD IN RIO DE JANEIRO IN 1992

The United Nations Earth Summit held in Rio de Janeiro in 1992 resulted in Agenda 21, a comprehensive plan of action for sustainable development. The Summit also led to the creation of important environmental agreements such as the Framework Convention on Climate Change and the Convention on Biological Diversity. The Millennium Development Goals (MDGs), established in 2000, further integrated sustainability into the global agenda by addressing poverty, education, gender equality, child mortality, maternal health, disease, environmental sustainability, and global partnerships. In 2015, the MDGs were succeeded by the Sustainable Development Goals (SDGs), a universal call to action to end poverty, protect the planet, and ensure prosperity for all. The SDGs expanded the scope of sustainable development, encompassing a broader range of issues, including climate change, clean energy, responsible consumption, and peace. Today, sustainable development is a guiding principle for governments, organizations, and communities worldwide.

3.05. Sustainable Development, The Relationship Between Humanity and Nature

The preservation of human survival is linked to our interaction with the natural environment. Attaining a sustainable way of life hinges on striking a delicate equilibrium between human consumption and the Earth's capacity for regeneration. However, despite this interdependence, there is a tendency for humans to behave as if they exist apart from nature.[169] Throughout the ages, mankind has, for economic and other reasons, constantly interfered with nature. In the past this was often done without consideration of the effects upon the environment. Owing to new scientific

[168] World Commission on Environment and Development. Our Common Future. Oxford University Press, 1987, p. 13.

[169] Schultz, P.W. (2002). Inclusion with Nature: The Psychology of Human-Nature Relations. In: Schmuck, P., Schultz, W.P. (eds) Psychology of Sustainable Development. Springer, Boston, MA.

insights and to a growing awareness of the risks for mankind for present and future generations.[170] An environment degraded by pollution and defaced by the destruction of all beauty and variety is as contrary to satisfactory living conditions and the development as the breakdown of the fundamental ecologic equilibria is harmful to physical and moral health.[171] Sustainable development embodies a visionary approach that seeks to harmonize human progress with the preservation of the environment and the well-being of future generations. This concept revolves around the idea of meeting the needs of the present without compromising the ability of future generations to meet their own needs. The path to sustainable development is however coupled with challenges. Economic, political, technological, and social obstacles that pose significant roadblocks. As we confront the realities of climate change, resource depletion, and social inequities, the imperative for action becomes undeniable.

3.06.CAUSES AND CONSEQUENCES OF CLIMATE CHANGE

Climate change, driven by human-induced factors, is reshaping the world as we know it. Understanding the causes and impacts of this phenomenon is paramount to mitigating its effects and fostering resilience in the face of environmental challenges. By unraveling the threads of climate change, we can comprehend its origins, recognize its consequences, and work toward sustainable solutions.

a.) Greenhouse Gas Emissions: -The primary cause of climate change is the increased concentration of greenhouse gases (GHGs) in the atmosphere. Activities such as burning fossil fuels, deforestation, and industrial processes release carbon dioxide (CO_2), methane (CH_4), and nitrous oxide (N_2O). These gases trap heat, creating a greenhouse effect that leads to a rise in global temperatures.

b.) Deforestation and Land Use Changes: - Deforestation, driven by agriculture, logging, and urbanization, reduces the Earth's capacity to absorb CO_2. Forests act as carbon sinks, sequestering carbon from the atmosphere. Land use changes and habitat destruction disrupt ecosystems, leading to imbalances in biodiversity and ecosystem services, amplifying climate change impacts.

c.) Natural Factors: - Natural factors, such as volcanic eruptions and solar radiation, influence the Earth's climate. Additionally, feedback loops, like melting Arctic ice reducing the Earth's

---

[170] Hungary v Slovakia), 1997 WL 1168556 (ICJ
171 Dinah L. Shelton & Alex Kiss, Guide to

International Environmental Law in Alexandre Kiss, Dinah Shelton, Guide to International Environmental Law (Martinus Nijhoff Publishers, 2007).

albedo (reflectivity), exacerbate warming. These interconnected processes can amplify climate change, triggering further environmental imbalances.

d.) Rising Global Temperatures: - Climate change leads to a steady increase in global temperatures. Warming contributes to more frequent and intense heatwaves, altering weather patterns, disrupting agricultural cycles, and threatening human health. Rising temperatures exacerbate water scarcity, impacting both agriculture and freshwater ecosystems.

e.) Melting Ice Caps and Rising Sea Levels:-One of the visible impacts of climate change is the melting of polar ice caps and glaciers. This phenomenon contributes to rising sea levels, posing a threat to coastal communities, infrastructure, and biodiversity-rich coastal habitats. Sea-level rise exacerbates the risk of flooding, especially in low-lying regions.

f.) Extreme Weather Events: - Climate change intensifies extreme weather events, including hurricanes, droughts, floods, and wildfires. These events have devastating consequences on human populations, agriculture, and natural habitats. Increased frequency and intensity of extreme weather events strain emergency response systems and disrupt societal stability.

g.) Biodiversity Loss and Ecosystem Disruption: -Climate change accelerates biodiversity loss by altering habitats, affecting migration patterns, and disrupting ecosystems. Species unable to adapt or migrate face extinction. Ecosystem disruption impacts pollination, soil fertility, and food chains, threatening both human food security and natural ecosystems.

h.) Ocean Acidification and Coral Bleaching: - Elevated CO_2 levels are absorbed by oceans, causing ocean acidification. Acidification harms marine life, particularly organisms with calcium carbonate shells or skeletons. Coral reefs, vital marine ecosystems, are vulnerable to bleaching due to rising sea temperatures, jeopardizing the livelihoods of coastal communities and marine biodiversity.

3.07. IMPORTANCE OF SUSTAINABLE DEVELOPMENT ON ENVIRONMENTAL MANAGEMENT

The World Commission on Environment and Development noted as follows: "We borrow environmental capital from future generations with no intention or prospect of repaying. We act as we do because we can get away with it: future generations do not vote; they have no political or financial power; they cannot challenge our decisions." [172] Environmental considerations have therefore had an impact on the agenda of many inter-national organizations. Environmental considerations affect various areas of the economy including all sorts of development projects, agriculture and forestry.[173] The consequences of rapid economic growth and development as an essential pointer of progress in modern society and the quest to become technologically advanced has put a lot of pressure on the environment as well as to the humans. The Sustained exploitation of natural resources and raw materials to support industry and human life has coupled the pressure on resources such as water land and air.

3.07. IMPORTANCE OF SUSTAINABLE DEVELOPMENT

The four recurring elements that comprise the concept of 'sustainable development' is the need to preserve natural resources for the benefit of future generations (the principle of intergenerational equity); exploiting natural resources in a manner which is 'sustainable', 'prudent', 'rational', 'wise' or 'appropriate' (the principle of sustainable use); the 'equitable' use of natural resources, and the need to ensure that environmental considerations are integrated into economic and other development plans, Programmes and projects, (the principle of integration).[174] Based upon the four elements sustainable development has the following ecological benefits.

1. Preservation of Ecosystems and Biodiversity: Sustainable development ensures the conservation of ecosystems and biodiversity, preserving essential natural resources for future generations.[175] Sustainable development recognizes the importance of ecosystem services (such as clean water, pollination, and soil fertility) for human well-being, emphasizing their conservation[176]

2. Climate Change Mitigation and Adaptation: Sustainable practices reduce greenhouse gas emissions, mitigating climate change effects and aiding communities in adapting to

---

[172] John Muthui & 19 others v County Government of Kitui & 7 others [2020] eKLR Para 84

[173] International Environmental Law-Fairness, Effectiveness, and World Order" by Elli Louka, Page 15. Para 1.

[174] Cullet P., Differential Treatment in International Environmental Law and its Contribution to the Evolution of International Law (Aldershot: Ashgate, 2003) pp 8-9).

[175] Convention on Biological Diversity. "Sustainable Development Goals." cbd.int, 2020.

[176] Daily, G. C. (1997). Nature's services: Societal dependence on natural ecosystems. Island Press.

environmental challenges.[177] By promoting sustainable economic practices, countries can achieve long-term economic stability, reducing the risks associated with resource depletion and environmental degradation.[178]

3.   **Poverty Alleviation and Social Equity:** Sustainable development promotes economic growth, providing opportunities for impoverished communities and fostering social equity.[179] Through sustainable development, poverty can be alleviated by providing equal access to resources, education, and healthcare, creating opportunities for impoverished populations.[180]

4.   **Resource Efficiency and Conservation:** Sustainable practices emphasize efficient resource use, minimizing waste and ensuring the longevity of finite resources[181] Sustainable practices address climate change by reducing greenhouse gas emissions, promoting renewable energy sources, and implementing energy-efficient technologies.[182]

5. **Promoting Clean Energy Sources:** Sustainable development encourages the adoption of renewable energy sources, reducing dependency on fossil fuels and mitigating environmental degradation.[183] Sustainable practices address climate change by reducing greenhouse gas emissions, promoting renewable energy sources, and implementing energy-efficient technologies.[184]

6.   **Ensuring Food Security:** Sustainable agricultural practices guarantee food security by maintaining soil fertility, conserving water, and promoting biodiversity in farming systems.[185]

[177] Intergovernmental Panel on Climate Change. *Global Warming of 1.5°C. Special Report.* IPCC, 2018.

[178] Pearce, D., & Barbier, E. B. (2000). Blueprint for a sustainable economy. Earthscan Publications.

[179] United Nations Development Programme. *Human Development Report 2019: Beyond income, beyond averages, beyond today: Inequalities in human development in the 21st century.* UNDP, 2019.

[180] Sachs, J. (2005). The End of Poverty: Economic Possibilities for Our Time. Penguin Books. [181] United Nations Environment Programme. *Global Resources Outlook 2019: Natural Resources for the Future We Want.* UNEP, 2018.

[182] Intergovernmental Panel on Climate Change (IPCC). (2014). Climate Change 2014: Mitigation of Climate Change. Cambridge University Press

[183] International Energy Agency. *Global Energy Review 2021.* IEA, 2021.

[184] Sustainable practices address climate change by reducing greenhouse gas emissions, promoting renewable energy sources, and implementing energy-efficient technologies

[185] Food and Agriculture Organization of the United Nations. The State of Food Security and Nutrition in the World 2020. FAO, 2020.

Encouraging sustainable consumption patterns and responsible production methods reduces waste and conserves resources, contributing to sustainable development goals.[186]

7. **Enhancing Water Management:** Sustainable development focuses on efficient water management, ensuring access to clean water for all while preserving aquatic ecosystems.[187] Sustainable development recognizes the importance of ecosystem services (such as clean water, pollination, and soil fertility) for human well-being, emphasizing their conservation.[188]

8. **Promoting Sustainable Urbanization:** Sustainable urban planning reduces pollution, promotes green spaces, and enhances public transportation, creating livable cities for present and future generations.[189] International collaboration and partnerships are essential for sustainable development, fostering knowledge exchange, technology transfer, and collective efforts to address global challenges.[190]

9. **Preservation of Cultural Heritage:** Sustainable development safeguards cultural heritage by promoting eco-friendly tourism, preserving historical sites, and ensuring the well-being of indigenous communities.[191] Sustainable development supports the preservation of cultural heritage and indigenous knowledge, respecting diverse traditions and customs.[192]

10. **Global Partnerships for Sustainable Development:** International collaboration and partnerships are vital for sustainable development, fostering knowledge exchange, technology transfer,

and financial support for developing nations. International collaboration and partnerships are essential for sustainable development, fostering knowledge exchange, technology transfer, and collective efforts to address global challenges.[193]

[186] United Nations (UN). (2015). Transforming our world: The 2030 Agenda for Sustainable Development.

[187] UN-Water. *Integrated Monitoring Guide for SDG 6: Targets and global indicators.* UN-Water, 2018.

[188] Daily, G. C. (1997). Nature's services: Societal dependence on natural ecosystems. Island Press.

[189] United Nations Human Settlements Programme. *The State of the World's Cities 2018.* UN- Habitat, 2019.

[190] United Nations Development Programme (UNDP). (2008). Human Development Report 2007/2008: Fighting climate change: Human solidarity in a divided world.

[191] United Nations Educational, Scientific and Cultural Organization. *World Heritage and Sustainable Development: The Role of Local Communities.* UNESCO, 2017.

[192] United Nations Educational, Scientific and Cultural Organization (UNESCO). (2003). Convention for the Safeguarding of the Intangible Cultural Heritage.

[193] United Nations Development Programme (UNDP). (2008). Human Development Report 2007/2008: Fighting climate change: Human solidarity in a divided world

3.08: ROLE OF SUSTAINABEL DEVELPMENT IN CLIMAT E CHANGE MITIGATION

Sustainable development plays a pivotal role in climate change mitigation, offering a holistic approach that addresses environmental, social, and economic dimensions. By promoting sustainable practices, societies can reduce greenhouse gas emissions, enhance resilience, and foster a low-carbon future. Understanding the intricate interplay between sustainable development and climate change mitigation is essential for building a resilient and equitable world.

1. **Promoting Renewable Energy Sources:** -Sustainable development encourages the widespread adoption of renewable energy sources such as solar, wind, and hydroelectric power. By investing in clean energy technologies, societies reduce dependence on fossil fuels, mitigating emissions and transitioning toward a low-carbon energy landscape.

2. **Encouraging Energy Efficiency:** -Sustainable development initiatives prioritize energy efficiency in industries, transportation, and buildings. Implementing energy-efficient technologies and practices reduces energy consumption, lowering emissions and operational costs while promoting a greener economy.

3. **Supporting Green Urban Planning:** -Sustainable urban development emphasizes green spaces, public transportation, and energy-efficient buildings. Compact, well-planned cities reduce the need for extensive commuting, curbing emissions, conserving resources, and enhancing the overall quality of life.

4. **Advocating Sustainable Agriculture:** -Promoting sustainable agricultural practices, including organic farming, agroforestry, and soil conservation, ensures food security while minimizing emissions from agriculture. Sustainable agriculture also enhances soil health, sequesters carbon, and preserves biodiversity.

5. **Conserving and Restoring Ecosystems:** -Sustainable

development initiatives focus on conserving natural ecosystems such as forests, wetlands, and mangroves. These ecosystems act as carbon sinks, absorbing CO_2 and mitigating climate change. Restoring degraded ecosystems enhances their carbon sequestration capacity and promotes biodiversity.

6. Fostering Climate-Resilient Communities: -Sustainable development builds climate-resilient communities by integrating climate adaptation measures into development projects. This includes constructing climate-resilient infrastructure, developing early warning systems, and enhancing community education and preparedness.

7. Promoting Circular Economy: -Sustainable development embraces the circular economy model, where resources are reused, recycled, and repurposed. By reducing waste and promoting sustainable consumption patterns, societies minimize emissions associated with production and disposal processes.

8.   Advancing Green Technologies: -Sustainable development encourages research and innovation in green technologies. From electric vehicles to carbon capture and storage systems, these technologies offer sustainable alternatives, reducing emissions in various sectors.

9.   Ensuring Social Equity and Environmental Justice: -Sustainable development prioritizes social equity and environmental justice, ensuring that vulnerable communities have access to resources, opportunities, and protection against climate impacts. Inclusive policies and community engagement empower marginalized populations to adapt and thrive amidst changing climate conditions.

3.09. THE SUSTAINABILITY OF NATURAL RESOURCES AND LEGISLATIVE POLICY

Sustainable Development is one of the national values and principles of governance in the Constitution that bind all State organs, State officers, public officers and all persons.[194] Sustainable development is a principle with a normative value, demanding a balance between development and environmental protection, and as a principle of reconciliation in the context of conflicting human rights, that is the right to development and the right to protecting the environment.[195] The Sustainability of natural resources requires urgent implementation of sound legislative and economic policies including the principles of international environmental law, particularly the principles of sustainable development, precaution, common but differentiated responsibilities, and inter and intra- generational equity, that constitute the fundamental part of the conceptual architecture of international environmental law.[196] This is critical in the implementation of agenda that align with environmental goals and to ensure that state parties and private entities do not inordinately exploit the environment in a manner that degrades the environment and our natural heritage without replenishing it or implementing any plans for future generations to benefit from our environment. The principles of international environmental law, particularly the principles of sustainable development, precaution, common but differentiated responsibilities, and inter and

194 Constitution of Kenya 2010, Article 10
195 John Muthui & 19 others v County Government of Kitui &
7 others [2020] eKLR Para 129
196 Philippe Sands and Jacqueline Peel, Principles
of International Environmental Law (4th Edition,
CUP 2018) 197– 251.

intra- generational equity, are a fundamental part of the conceptual architecture of international environmental law.[197]

3.10. Key Principles of Sustainable Development

a) Interconnectedness of Environmental, Social, and Economic Factors.

The concept of sustainable development rests on the recognition of the elaborate web that links environmental, social, and economic factors. Understanding the profound interconnections among these elements is pivotal for crafting holistic and effective strategies to ensure a balanced and sustainable future. Environmental factors, such as climate change and natural resource availability, have direct implications on both social well-being and economic stability. Extreme weather events and resource depletion can lead to displacement, food insecurity, and economic downturns, underscoring the intimate link between environmental challenges and human societies' resilience and prosperity. Social factors, including cultural norms, education, and public awareness, play a vital role in shaping environmental attitudes and behaviors. Examining how societal values influence conservation efforts, environmental education, and community engagement provides insights into the dynamics that drive sustainable practices at the grassroots level.

Economic models and policies significantly impact natural ecosystems and biodiversity. Capitalism, socialism, and other economic paradigms have varying effects on resource utilization, pollution levels, and environmental preservation efforts. Analyzing these relationships sheds light on the need for sustainable economic practices, circular economies, and green innovations to mitigate ecological harm.

3.ADAPTATION STRATEGIES: BUILDING RESILIENCE TO CLIMATE IMPACTS

a) **Climate-Resilient Infrastructure:-**Designing infrastructure that can withstand extreme weather events, such as resilient buildings and flood-resistant roads, protects communities from climate-related disasters.

b) **Early Warning Systems:-**Developing and enhancing early warning systems for extreme weather events helps communities prepare and evacuate, reducing the impact of disasters.

c) **Climate-Smart Agriculture:-**Implementing climate-smart agricultural techniques, such as drought-resistant crops and efficient water management, ensures food security amidst changing climate patterns.

---

[197] Ibidem

d) **Ecosystem-Based Adaptation:** -Preserving and restoring natural ecosystems, such as mangroves and wetlands, provides natural buffers against climate-related hazards like storm surges and flooding.

e) **Community Engagement and Education:** - Educating communities about climate risks and involving them in adaptation planning enhances local resilience and fosters a sense of collective responsibility.

3.18. Integrated Strategies

a.) Nature-Based Solutions: -Utilizing nature-based solutions, like reforestation and restoring degraded ecosystems, not only sequesters carbon but also enhances biodiversity and provides adaptation benefits.

b. Inclusive and Equitable Policies:-Developing policies that prioritize vulnerable communities ensures equity in adaptation efforts, leaving no one behind in the face of climate impacts.

c). International Collaboration: -Collaborating globally on technology transfer, climate finance, and knowledge sharing enables nations to pool resources and expertise, enhancing collective resilience and mitigation efforts. Mitigation and adaptation strategies are interconnected components of a comprehensive climate action plan. By integrating these strategies, societies can navigate the challenges of climate change, reduce vulnerabilities, and work towards a sustainable future where the adverse impacts of climate change are minimized, and communities thrive in harmony with their environment.

3.11. SOCIAL EQUITY AS A PILLAR OF SUSTAINABLE DEVELOPMENT

Social equity, encompassing issues of gender, race, and income disparities, is indispensable for sustainable development. Examining how marginalized communities bear the brunt of environmental degradation and exploring strategies for inclusive environmental policies and resource distribution is crucial. Ensuring that the benefits of sustainable initiatives are accessible to all fosters social cohesion and environmental justice. The challenge lies in balancing economic growth with environmental preservation. Economic activities often exert pressure on natural resources and ecosystems. Delving into sustainable business practices, green technologies, and corporate social responsibility initiatives highlights the ways in which businesses can contribute positively to the environment while remaining economically viable.

3.12.THE PRECAUTIONARY PRINCIPLE

The precautionary principle stands as one of the fundamental tenets of international environmental law. Serving as a symbol of "technical democracy," this principle has been a cornerstone of the Rio Declaration, marking the beginning of a broad and rapid evolution of precautionary approaches that now underpin many legal systems. Through constructive dialogue, international courts have progressively emphasized the precautionary principle, delving into its authority, contents, and implications. Its intricate and multifaceted nature remains a challenge, yet in today's societies marked by continuous technical innovation, its incorporation into positive law appears irresistible. Judges are anticipated to play a pivotal role in shaping the development of this "open textured" standard. [198]

The precautionary principle, a cornerstone of environmental conservation, embodies the ethos of erring on the side of caution in the face of uncertainty. It asserts that if an action, policy, or technology has the potential to cause harm to the public or the environment, in the absence of scientific consensus, the burden of proof falls on those advocating for the action. Understood as a preventive approach, the precautionary principle places significant importance on long-term environmental sustainability. Examining this principle in the context of environmental conservation reveals its transformative power in shaping policies and practices that prioritize the preservation of our natural heritage. The precautionary principle emphasizes proactive measures even when conclusive scientific evidence is lacking. By avoiding potentially harmful activities or substances, environmental conservation efforts prevent irreversible damage to ecosystems, wildlife, and human health, safeguarding the delicate balance of nature.

A.) ENVIRONMENTAL IMPACT ASSESSMENTS AND DECISION MAKING:

Environmental Impact Assessment (EIA) is a systematic process used to identify, predict, evaluate, and mitigate the environmental effects of proposed projects, policies, or plans. It provides valuable information to decision-makers, allowing them to make informed choices that balance development with environmental preservation.[199] Environmental impact assessments (EIAs) serve as practical applications of the precautionary principle. By conducting thorough assessments before initiating projects, policymakers and stakeholders can evaluate potential risks, allowing

[198] Yann Kerbrat, Sandrine Maljean-Dubois. The Role of International Law in the Promotion of the Precautionary Principle. Carina Costa de Oliveira, Gabriela G. B. Lima Moraes, Fabrício Ramos Ferreira (dir.), A interpretação do princípio da precaução no direito brasileiro, no direito comparado e no direito internacional, Pontes, pp. 275-284, 2019. ffhalshs-02342746f

[199] Sadler, B. (1996). International Study of the Effectiveness of Environmental Assessment. Environmental Impact Assessment Review, 16(1), 5-21.

informed decisions that minimize adverse effects on the environment. This process ensures that proposed activities align with conservation objectives. EIAs provide decision-makers with comprehensive information about the potential environmental consequences of various options, enabling them to make environmentally responsible choices.[200]

B.) BIODIVERSITY CONSERVATION AND HABITAT PROTECTION:

The precautionary principle underscores the importance of preserving biodiversity and protecting natural habitats. Conservation initiatives guided by this principle focus on maintaining the diverse array of species and ecosystems. By safeguarding biodiversity, ecosystems remain resilient, ensuring their ability to adapt to changing environmental conditions. Biodiversity conservation and habitat protection are critical components of environmental sustainability. Biodiversity conservation ensures the preservation of various species and ecosystems, which in turn provide essential services such as clean water, pollination, and climate regulation, benefiting both human populations and wildlife.[201] Biodiversity, the variety of life forms on Earth, and ecosystem services, the benefits humans obtain from ecosystems, are essential components of our planet's health and prosperity. Conservation efforts directed toward preserving biodiversity and ecosystem services are critical for maintaining ecological balance, ensuring human well-being, and fostering sustainable development. Examining this topic sheds light on the intricate relationships between ecosystems, biodiversity, and human societies, highlighting the urgency of conservation initiatives.

1. **Biodiversity as a Pillar of Stability:** - Biodiversity acts as a foundation for ecosystem stability. Diverse ecosystems are more resilient to environmental changes, making them better equipped to withstand disturbances such as climate change, diseases, and natural disasters. Conservation

of various species and genetic diversity within ecosystems ensures their adaptive capacity and long-term sustainability.

2.   Ecosystem   Services: Nature's Contributions to Humanity: -Ecosystem services encompass a wide array of benefits, including clean water, pollination, climate regulation, and disease control, which directly impact human well-being. By conserving ecosystems, societies secure these vital services, supporting agriculture, human health, and economic activities.

---

[200] Glasson, J., Therivel, R., & Chadwick, A. (2012). Introduction to Environmental Impact Assessment. Routledge.

[201] Millennium Ecosystem Assessment (MEA). (2005). Ecosystems and Human Well-being: Biodiversity Synthesis. World Resources Institute.

Understanding the tangible benefits derived from intact ecosystems emphasizes their intrinsic value and the need for conservation efforts.

3. **Biodiversity and Cultural Significance:** - Biodiversity holds cultural significance for many indigenous communities and societies worldwide. Conservation efforts not only preserve unique species but also protect cultural heritage and traditional knowledge. Recognizing the cultural importance of biodiversity fosters respect for nature and strengthens the connection between communities and their natural surroundings.

4. **Threats to Biodiversity: Human Impact and Climate Change:** -Human activities, including deforestation, habitat destruction, pollution, and overexploitation, pose significant threats to biodiversity. Climate change exacerbates these challenges, altering habitats and disrupting ecosystems. Analyzing the impact of these threats highlights the urgent need for conservation strategies, emphasizing the role of sustainable practices, habitat restoration, and pollution control.

5. **Conservation Strategies: Preserving Biodiversity and Ecosystem Services:** - Conservation strategies encompass a range of approaches, from protected area management and wildlife corridors to reforestation and sustainable agriculture practices. Integrating biodiversity conservation into urban planning and promoting sustainable resource use are essential components. Collaboration between governments, communities, and organizations is crucial for effective conservation initiatives, ensuring the preservation of biodiversity and the services it provides.

6. **Economic Value of Biodiversity and Ecosystem Services:** -Biodiversity and

ecosystem services contribute significantly to economies. Ecosystem-based industries, ecotourism, and pharmaceuticals derived from natural sources are integral to the global economy. By conserving biodiversity, societies sustain these economic avenues, emphasizing the economic value of conservation and encouraging responsible practices for long-term economic benefits. Conservation of biodiversity and ecosystem services is not only a scientific necessity but also a moral imperative. As societies recognize the intricate web linking biodiversity, ecosystems, and human well-being, prioritizing conservation becomes paramount.

C.)CLIMATE CHANGE MITIGATION AND ADAPTATION:

Mitigation refers to efforts and strategies aimed at reducing or preventing the emission of greenhouse gases (GHGs) and minimizing human-induced climate change. In the face of climate change, the precautionary principle drives efforts to mitigate greenhouse gas emissions and adapt to the changing climate. By reducing emissions, conserving forests, and promoting sustainable practices, societies mitigate potential future environmental catastrophes. Moreover, adaptation strategies, such as building resilient infrastructure, are essential in the face of uncertain climate impacts. Mitigation efforts focus on reducing emissions from various sectors such as energy, transportation, industry, and agriculture. This includes transitioning to renewable energy sources, improving energy efficiency, and promoting sustainable agricultural practices[202]

d.) Sustainable Technology Development and Innovation:

Sustainable technology development and innovation refer to the process of creating new technologies or improving existing ones in a way that addresses environmental, social, and economic challenges while promoting long-term sustainability. The precautionary principle guides the development and deployment of new technologies. By prioritizing the safety of innovations, society can embrace sustainable technologies, such as renewable energy sources and eco-friendly materials. Responsible technological advancement ensures that human progress aligns harmoniously with environmental conservation goals. The precautionary principle serves as a guiding light in the realm of environmental conservation, urging humanity to tread lightly, think long-term, and prioritize the well-being of our planet. By integrating this principle into decision- making processes, societies worldwide can embark on a collective journey toward a more sustainable and ecologically balanced future.

[202] Intergovernmental Panel on Climate Change (IPCC). (2014). Climate Change 2014: Mitigation of Climate Change. Cambridge University Press.

3.13. The Legal Infrastructure for Sustainable Development Under Kenya's Law. The quality of life for the future generation depends on our decisions today. The need for change in human development for them to lead happy lives has been debated for decades. The sustainability discourse started in the 1970s, and the 1992 UN Conference on the Environment and Development recognized intergenerational equity as central for policymaking that safeguards the future - this principle is now found in the constitutions of many countries, including Kenya. [203] Kenya, like many other countries, has established a legal framework to support sustainable development. The legal infrastructure for sustainable development in Kenya is based on a combination of national laws, regulations, policies, and international agreements.

1.CONSTITUTION OF KENYA (2010)

The Kenyan Constitution, adopted in 2010, includes provisions related to environmental conservation, land use planning, and natural resource management. The principle behind the law permitting any person to institute a suit relating to the protection of the environment without the necessity of demonstrating personal loss or injury is because the protection of the environment is not only for the benefit of the present generation, but also for the future generation.

•THE PREAMBLE TO THE CONSTITUTION

The preamble to the Constitution recognizes the importance of protecting the environment for the benefit of the future generation as follows "Respectful of the environment, which is our heritage, and determined to sustain it for the benefit of future generations."

- **ARTICLE 69 OF THE CONSTITUTION**

Article 69 of the Constitution, for example, emphasizes the need to ensure sustainable exploitation, utilization, management, and conservation of the environment and natural resources. The court has held that Article 42 of the Constitution guarantees every person the right to a clean and healthy environment and to have the environment protected for the benefit of present and future generations through the measures prescribed by Article 69. The right extends to having the obligations relating to the environment under Article 70 fulfilled.[204] Article 70 of the Constitution grants any person the right to commence proceedings for the enforcement of the right to a clean

[203] John Muthui & 19 others v County Government of Kitui & 7 others [2020] eKLR Para 84.
[204] Adrian Kamotho Njenga vs. Council of Governors & 3 others [2020] eKLR

and healthy environment. The said Article provides that "If a person alleges that a right to a clean and healthy environment recognized and protected under Article 42 has been, is being or is likely to be, denied, violated, infringed or threatened, the person may apply to a court for redress in addition to any other legal remedies that are available in respect to the same matter.[205] For the purposes of this Article, an applicant does not have to demonstrate that any person has incurred loss or suffered injury."[206] This position was in fact the applicable position, and still is the position, under the Environmental Coordination and Management Act (EMCA), 1999, which preceded the Constitution of Kenya, 2010. Section 3(4) above permits any person to institute suit relating to the protection of the environment without the necessity of demonstrating personal loss or injury

2.WILDLIFE CONSERVATION AND MANAGEMENT ACT (2013)

This Act aims to conserve wildlife and their habitats, regulate wildlife-related activities, and promote community involvement in wildlife conservation efforts. It establishes the legal framework for sustainable wildlife management in the country.

3.WATER ACT (2016)

This Act governs the management and use of water resources in Kenya. It promotes sustainable water use, conservation, and allocation, emphasizing community participation and the protection of water sources.

4. FORESTRY ACT (2020):

The Forestry Act provides a legal framework for the sustainable management, conservation, and utilization of forests and forest resources in Kenya. It addresses issues such as tree planting, logging, and forest conservation efforts.

5. WILDLIFE CONSERVATION AND MANAGEMENT ACT (2013)

This Act aims to conserve wildlife and their habitats, regulate wildlife-related activities, and promote community involvement in wildlife conservation efforts. It establishes the legal framework for sustainable wildlife management in the country.

6.LAND ACT (2012)

The Land Act provides regulations related to land tenure, land use planning, and management. It promotes secure land rights, equitable access to land, and sustainable land use practices.

7. ENERGY ACT (2019)

This Act addresses various aspects of the energy sector, including renewable energy development, energy efficiency, and environmental safeguards. It promotes the use of clean and renewable energy sources.

8.CLIMATE CHANGE ACT (2016)

The Climate Change Act provides a framework for addressing climate change issues in Kenya. It establishes the legal basis for climate change adaptation and mitigation strategies, including the development of a national climate change action plan.

9. The Environmental Management and Coordination Act.

Indeed, Section 18 of the Environment and Land Court Act and Section 3(5) of the Environmental Management and Co-ordination Act provides that The Environment and Land's Court should be guided by the principle of *intergenerational* equity while resolving environmental disputes. Section 2 of the Environmental Management and Coordination Act defines intergenerational Equity as follows: "intergenerational equity" means that the present generation should ensure that in exercising its rights to beneficial use of the environment the health, diversity and productivity of the environment is maintained or enhanced for the benefit of future generations."[207]

3.14. THE PRINCIPLES OF SUSTAINABLE ENVIRONMENTAL MANAGEMENT

The concept of sustainable development embodies eight novel principles, they include the Polluter Pays Principle, The Precautionary Principle, The Intergenerational Equity Principle, The Public Participation Principle and The Environmental Impact Assessment Principle. These novel principles provide the foundation for meeting the obligations towards the environment for sustainable development. The principles of sustainable development now form provisions of law and policy and have the force of law. Some important aspects of these principles that extend liability to persons and entities that destroy the environment are included in the polluter pays principle.

1. **The Polluter-Pays Principle**. -The polluter pays principle embodies an approach that places the economic costs of polluting the environment upon the parties that pollute the environment. While Environmental pollution ultimately remains an inevitable problem, the

---

[207] Section 18 of the Environment and Land Court Act

mitigation of hazardous action over the environment is possible, economic progress and industrial activity no doubt generate waste that must ultimately be disposed of. By disposing the waste in the environment, the polluting entity must be wary of the effect and hazard the pollution will cause to the surrounding ecosystem. Regarding the first principle of polluter pays, it is necessary to use the term to cover obligation on any person to conduct their affairs in an environmentally sympathetic fashion, anyone conducting activity ought to be aware of and accept responsibility for the environmental consequences of that activity, with regards to sustainable development. The Constructive view of the phrase should be that present development should meet the needs of the present without compromising the ability of future generation to meet their own needs. (hence intergenerational equity and intergenerational equity). For the best practicable means, one would like to consider whether one has or can do what is practicable in terms of prevention or reduction where the defendant has discharged the obligation bestowed

on him the nuisance or pollution may continue.[208] This principle embodies the viewpoint that the costs of cleaning up any element of the environment damaged by pollution, compensating victims of pollution, cost of beneficial uses lost as a result of an act of pollution and other costs that are connected with or incidental to the polluters actions, must be paid or borne by the person that pollutes the environment.

- **Aspects of The Polluter Pays Principle Under Kenyan Legislation.**
    - a) **Spillers liability:** - Section 93 of the

Environmental Management and Co-Ordination Act Prohibits the discharge of hazardous substances, chemicals, and materials such as polluting motor oil into the environment. The section also emphasizes on the spiller's liability. The Act prohibits the discharge any hazardous substance, chemical, oil or mixture containing oil into any waters or any other segments of the environment. The Act stipulates that a person who discharges a hazardous substance, chemical, oil or a mixture containing oil into any waters or other segments of the environment commits an offence and in addition to any other sentence imposed by the court a spillers liability should be imposed upon the person to pay for the cost of the removal of the hazardous substance, chemical, oil or a mixture containing oil including any costs which may be incurred by any Government agency or organ in the restoration of the environment damaged or destroyed as a result of the discharge.

b) Extension of liability to third party costs: - The liability extends to the costs of third parties in the form of reparation, restoration, restitution, or compensation as may be determined by

[208] Environmental Law by John Dleeson page 34

a competent court on application by such third parties. The owner or operator of a production or storage facility, motor vehicle or vessel from which a discharge occurs is also required to mitigate the impact of the discharge by giving immediate notice of the discharge to the Authority and other relevant Government officers; immediately beginning clean-up operations using the best available clean-up methods. If the owner or operator of a production or storage facility, motor vehicle or vessel refuses, neglects or fails to take the mitigation measures as required above, The National Environmental Management Authority is authorized to seize the polluting production or storage facility, motor vehicle or vessel, which it may after reasonable time, dispose of, to meet the costs of taking the necessary measures and other remedial and restoration measures.[209]

2. THE PRE CAUTIONARY PRINCIPLE.

This principle embodies a preventative or preventive approach, the philosophy behind this principle is the mitigation of pollution and environmental destruction before it occurs. All acts that are presumably hazardous must be precluded as a precaution. The Environmental Management and Coordination Act explains the principle in the diction that, 'where there are threats of damage to the environment, whether serious or irreversible, lack of full scientific certainty should not preclude or be used as a reason for postponing cost-effective measures to prevent environmental degradation.'[210] The precautionary principle is incorprated in Kenya's environmental law by way of mandatory Environmental Audit and Monitoring under The Environmental Management and Coordination Act. The law tasks the National Environmental Management Authority with the responsibility of undertaking constant environmental audit and monitoring to check all activities that are likely to have significant effect on the environment.[211]

---

[209] Section 93 of the Environmental Management and Co-Ordination Act.

[210] The Environmental Management and Co-Ordination Act Chapter 387, Revised Edition 2012

[1999] Page E12 – 14.

[211]Section 68 of The Environmental Management and Co-Ordination Act Chapter 387, Revised Edition 2012 [1999].

- **Provisions for The Precautionary Principle in Kenyan Legislation.**

a) Environmental Audit and Monitoring Mechanisms: -

To prevent degradation of the Environment, there are various provisions under the Environmental Management and Coordination Act that endeavor to uphold a precautionary approach towards environmental governance.

B) ENVIRONMENTAL AUDITING AND MONITORING

The Act provides for an Authority called an environmental inspector. [212] The officer is concerned with the role of auditing and monitoring environmental activities. The officer is empowered to enter any land or premises for the purposes of determining how far the activities carried out on that land or premises conform with the statements made in the environmental impact assessment study report issued in respect of that land or those premises under section 58(2).

C) ENVIRONMENTAL IMPACT ASSESSMENT RECORDS

The Environmental Management and Coordination Act requires the owners of the premises and the operator of a project for which an environmental impact assessment study report has been made to keep accurate records regarding the state of the environment. The owner has a mandate of making annual reports to the Authority describing how far the project conforms in operation with the statements made in the environmental impact assessment study report submitted under section 58(2) of the Environmental Management and Coordination Act. [213]

D) MITIGATION OF UNDESIRABLE EFFECTS BY OWNERS OF PREMISES

The Environmental Management and Coordination Act mandates occupiers and operators of projects to take all reasonable measures to mitigate any unforeseeable or undesirable effects that are not contemplated in the environmental impact assessment study report submitted as required under section 58(2) of the Act. The owner must further prepare and submit environmental audit reports on measures to the Authority annually or as the Authority might, in writing, require.[214]

E) ENVIRONMENTAL MONITORING.

The Environmental Management and Co-Ordination Act, tasks the National Environmental Management Authority in consultation with the relevant lead agencies to monitor all

[212] Section 68(2) of The Environmental Management and Coordination Act. [213] Section 68(3) of The Environmental Management and Coordination Act. [214] Section 68(4) of The Environmental Management and Coordination Act.

environmental phenomena with a view to [=;'/ assessing any possible changes in the environment and the possible impacts. The Authority also
monitors the operations of other industries and projects' activity with a view of determining the latter's immediate and long-term effects on the environment.[215]

3.INTERGENERATIONAL EQUITY PRINCIPLE.

Intergenerational equity" means that the present generation should ensure that in exercising its rights to beneficial use of the environment the health, diversity and productivity of the environment is maintained or enhanced for the benefit of future generations; "intergenerational equity" means that all people within the present generation have the right to benefit equally from the exploitation of the environment, and that they have an equal entitlement to a clean and healthy environment. intergenerational equity, the principle that current generations should ensure that natural resources are used sustainably, leaving a comparable or improved environmental state for future generations, as reflected in Kenya's legal framework.

•AN ENTITLEMENT OF PRESENT AND FUTURE GENERATIONS

The court has held that Unlike the other rights in the bill of rights of the Kenyan constitution which are guaranteed for enjoyment by individuals during their lifetime, the right to a clean and healthy environment is an entitlement of present and future generations and is to be enjoyed by every person with the obligation to conserve and protect the environment.

- **TRIPARTITE COMPONENTS**

The right has three components; the right itself, the right to have unrestricted access to the courts to seek redress where a person alleges the right to a clean and healthy environment has been infringed or is threatened; and the right to have the court make any order or give any directions it considers appropriate to either prevent or discontinue the act harmful to the environment, or compel any public officer to take measures to prevent or discontinue the act that is harmful to the environment or award compensation to any victim of a violation of the right to a clean and healthy environment."[216]

- **ENSURING EQUITABLE ACCESS AND BENEFIT SHARING**

The Constitution of Kenya (2010) underscores the importance of sustainable resource management for present and future generations. Article 69 specifically highlights the need to exploit, utilize,

---

[215] Section 69 of The Environmental Management and Coordination Act.

[216] Adrian Kamotho Njenga vs. Council of Governors & 3 others [2020] eKLR Para 19

manage, and conserve natural resources sustainably, ensuring equitable access and benefit-sharing among generations[217]. Additionally, the Environmental Management and Coordination Act (EMCA) of 1999 establishes guidelines for environmental conservation, considering the long-term well-being of future generations. These laws emphasize the responsibility of current generations to preserve the environment for the prosperity and livelihoods of future Kenyan citizens.[218]

A.) SOCIAL EQUITY AND JUSTICE IN DEVELOPMENT INITIATIVES

environmental actions and outcomes are strongly influenced by governance. Therefore, governance seems to be the most applicable answer to respond to the complicated, long-termed, multi-scaled, and multi-sectorial aspects of the environment.[219] Social equity and justice lie at the heart of sustainable development initiatives, emphasizing fair opportunities, equal access, and the elimination of disparities among diverse societal groups. In the context of development initiatives, these principles underscore the importance of inclusivity, community empowerment, and addressing historical inequalities. Environmental justice emphasizes the fair distribution of environmental benefits and burdens, ensuring that marginalized communities are not disproportionately affected by environmental hazards or deprived of access to natural resources. Social equity, on the other hand, encompasses broader notions of fairness and justice in society, including economic, political, and cultural dimensions.

b) . Inclusive Development Planning: - Inclusive development planning refers to the process of creating policies, programs, and initiatives that consider the needs and aspirations of all members of society, especially those who are marginalized or disadvantaged. It aims to promote social equity, equal opportunities, and active participation of diverse communities in the development process. Inclusive development planning involves active participation and engagement of all stakeholders, including vulnerable and marginalized groups. It ensures their involvement in decision-making processes, allowing them to voice their concerns and aspirations [220] Social equity in development begins with inclusive planning processes that actively involve marginalized communities, ensuring their voices are heard. By incorporating diverse perspectives,

[217] Constitution of Kenya (2010). Article 69. Nairobi: Government Printer.

[218] Environmental Management and Coordination Act (EMCA) of 1999. Laws of Kenya, Cap. 387A. Nairobi: Government Printer.

[219] Ogunkan, David V. "Achieving Sustainable Environmental Governance in Nigeria: A Review for Policy Consideration." Author Links Open Overlay Panel.

[220] Narayan, D. (1995). The contribution of people's participation: Evidence from 121 rural water supply projects. Environmentally Sustainable Development Occasional Paper Series, No. 1. The World Bank.

development initiatives can address specific needs, promote cultural sensitivity, and avoid unintended negative consequences, fostering a sense of ownership among all stakeholders.

c). **Equal Access to Basic Resources and Services:** - Inclusive planning focuses on providing equitable access to essential resources such as education, healthcare, clean water, and social services. It aims to bridge the gap between privileged and disadvantaged communities.[221] Development initiatives guided by social equity prioritize equal access to essential resources such as education, healthcare, clean water, and sanitation. By ensuring these services reach underserved populations, societies can bridge gaps, improve living standards, and enhance overall well-being, fostering a more just society.

d). **Gender Equality and Women's Empowerment:** - Inclusive development planning promotes gender equality by addressing disparities and ensuring equal opportunities for women and men. It involves policies that empower women, eliminate gender-based violence, and enhance women's economic participation.[222] Promoting gender equality is a fundamental aspect of social justice. Development initiatives should actively work towards empowering women, ensuring their participation in decision-making processes, providing access to education and healthcare, and creating opportunities for economic independence. Gender equality not only benefits women but also contributes significantly to the overall development of communities.

e). **Reducing Economic Disparities:** - Inclusive planning focuses on providing equitable access to essential resources such as education, healthcare, clean water, and social services. It aims to bridge the gap between privileged and disadvantaged communities.[223] Social equity initiatives focus on reducing economic disparities by providing skill development programs, vocational training, and access to credit and resources for marginalized communities. By promoting entrepreneurship and supporting small-scale enterprises, development efforts can uplift economically disadvantaged individuals, fostering economic resilience and self-sufficiency.

f). Environmental Justice and Community Resilience: - Inclusive planning respects and integrates diverse cultural perspectives. It acknowledges and incorporates traditional knowledge

[221] United Nations Development Programme (UNDP). (2019). Human Development Report 2019: Beyond income, beyond averages, beyond today: Inequalities in human development in the 21st century.

[222] Duflo, E. (2012). Women's empowerment and economic development. Journal of Economic Literature, 50(4), 1051-1079.

[223] United Nations Development Programme (UNDP). (2019). Human Development Report 2019: Beyond income, beyond averages, beyond today: Inequalities in human development in the 21st century.

and practices of indigenous communities, fostering cultural preservation and social cohesion.[224] Environmental justice emphasizes fair treatment and involvement of all communities in environmental decisions, addressing environmental issues and their health impacts. Development initiatives should prioritize vulnerable communities disproportionately affected by environmental hazards. By building community resilience, societies can withstand environmental challenges and create sustainable living environments.

g). **Education and Awareness Programs:** - Inclusive development planning includes capacity-building initiatives to enhance the skills and capabilities of marginalized communities. This empowerment enables them to actively participate in decision-making processes and improve their socio-economic status.[225] Education and awareness programs play a crucial role in promoting social equity. By providing education on rights, civic responsibilities, and environmental conservation, societies can empower individuals and communities to advocate for their needs, demand social justice, and actively participate in the development process.

h). **Social Safety Nets and Support Systems:** - Inclusive planning includes the establishment of social safety nets to protect vulnerable populations from economic shocks. These safety nets can include cash transfer programs, food assistance, and healthcare subsidies.[226] Development initiatives should establish social safety nets and support systems for vulnerable populations, ensuring access to healthcare, housing, and employment opportunities. By providing a safety net, societies can protect the most vulnerable members, fostering social stability and resilience against economic shocks.

3.15.INTEGRATION OF TRADITIONAL KNOWLEDGE AND MODERN SCIENCE

The integration of traditional knowledge and modern science represents a powerful synergy, merging ancient wisdom with contemporary advancements to address complex challenges. Traditional knowledge, passed down through generations, encompasses indigenous practices and insights derived from close interaction with the natural world. Modern science, on the other hand, offers systematic methodologies and innovative technologies. Together, they form a dynamic

---

[224] United Nations Educational, Scientific and Cultural Organization (UNESCO). (2006). Convention on the Diversity of Cultural Expressions.

[225] World Bank. (2005). Indigenous Peoples, Poverty, and Human Development in Latin America: 1994-2004. World Bank

[226] World Bank. (2015). The State of Social Safety Nets 2015. World Bank Group.

partnership, driving sustainable solutions and fostering harmonious coexistence between humanity and the environment.

1. **Preserving Indigenous Knowledge and Enhancing Environmental Stewardship.** Indigenous communities possess a wealth of knowledge about local ecosystems, biodiversity, and sustainable practices. Integrating this traditional wisdom into conservation efforts not only preserves cultural heritage but also offers invaluable insights into preserving natural resources and maintaining ecological balance. Traditional knowledge emphasizes the interconnectedness of all living beings and the environment. By incorporating these holistic perspectives into scientific research, modern science gains a deeper understanding of ecosystems. This enriched knowledge informs conservation strategies, enabling more effective environmental stewardship and sustainable resource management.

2. **Bridging Gaps in Scientific Understanding for Sustainable Agriculture and Food Security.**
Traditional knowledge often fills gaps in scientific knowledge, providing insights into subtle ecological and local adaptations. By recognizing and respecting indigenous knowledge, scientific research becomes more comprehensive and nuanced. This collaborative approach promotes mutual learning, bridging the divide between traditional wisdom and scientific understanding. Traditional agricultural practices, shaped by generations of observation and adaptation, offer valuable insights into sustainable farming techniques. Integrating these practices with modern agricultural innovations enhances crop resilience, reduces environmental impact, and ensures food security. By combining indigenous wisdom with modern agricultural science, societies can achieve sustainable food production.

3. **Ethnobotany and Medicinal Discoveries:** - Traditional knowledge about medicinal plants and herbal remedies has often led to the discovery of pharmaceutical

compounds. Ethnobotanical studies, which document traditional plant uses, provide a rich source of information for pharmaceutical research. This integration leads to the development of new medicines while respecting indigenous cultures and their contributions to healthcare.

4. **Climate Change Adaptation and Resilience:-** Indigenous communities, closely attuned to natural rhythms, possess adaptive strategies honed over centuries. Integrating these strategies with modern climate science enhances climate change adaptation efforts. Traditional practices such as water conservation, sustainable agriculture, and disaster preparedness serve as valuable models for building resilience in the face of climate-related challenges.

3.16. SUSTAINABLE DEVELOPMENT GOALS

Kenya in the quest to align its economic model with a sustainable agenda has endorsed the united Nations' sustainable development goals, Kenya specifically adopted Agenda 21 of the United Nations Conference on Environment and Development that was held in Rio De-janeiro Brazil, the agenda seeks to provide the world with solutions to the challenges associated with development and the environment. Kenya has also ratified major international agreements, treaties, conventions, and protocols resulting from the conference in harmony with the country's plans for sustainable development such as The United Nations Framework Convention on Climate Change that seeks to limit average global temperature increases and climate change, the United Nations Convention on Biological Diversity and the UN Convention to Combat Desertification as well as subsequent agreements that put in place active institutions to address climate change, biological diversity loss and combating of desertification by member countries.[227]

1.FOUNDATION OF KENYA'S ENVIRONMENTAL LEGISLATION AND POLICY

The foundation of Kenya's environmental policy is based on the Sustainable Development agenda that seeks to Protect our Planet and its natural resources and climate for future generations, to end poverty and hunger in all forms and ensure dignity and equality, to ensure prosperous and fulfilling lives in harmony with nature, and to foster peaceful, just and inclusive societies. The Sustainable Development Goals entail a universal agreement to end poverty and craft an equal, and secure world, the safety of the planet and our prosperity.

2. SUSTAINABLE DEVELOPMENT GOALS

a.) Harmonious existence of Humans with the environment.

Agenda 21 emphasizes the significance of the harmonious existence of humans alongside the environment by stressing on the need to Implement the sustainable development agenda through a solid global partnership that seeks to end poverty and hunger in all its forms everywhere in order to promote food security and improved nutrition as well as sustainable agriculture. This will ensure healthy lives that promotes the well-being for all at all ages.

---

[227] Sustainable Development in Kenya: Stocktaking in the run up to Rio+20

b.) Sustainable management of water and Access to affordable, reliable, sustainable, and modern energy.

The agenda also emphasizes on ensuring the availability and sustainable management of water and sanitation and access to affordable, reliable, sustainable and modern energy for all, ensuring sustainable consumption and production patterns as well as taking urgent action to combat climate change and its impacts by Conserving and sustainably utilizing the oceans, seas and marine resources for sustainable development, Protecting, restoring and promoting the sustainable use of terrestrial ecosystems, sustainably managing forests and combating desertification, as well as halting and reversing land degradation and halting biodiversity loss

c.) Peaceful and inclusive societies for sustainable development.

The principles of sustainable development also seek to promote peaceful and inclusive societies for sustainable development, with effective, accountable, and inclusive institutions at all levels that seeks to strengthen the means of implementation the Global Partnership for Sustainable Development. The principles of sustainable development guide policy makers in implementing decisions and the courts in exercising their authority on matters relating to the protection of the environment. These principles are provided for in the constitution of Kenya 2010 as well as other acts of parliament such as the Environmental Management and Coordination Act amongst other environmental regulations.

3.17.MITIGATION AND ADAPTATION STRATEGIES.

Mitigation involves reducing or preventing the emission of greenhouse gases, addressing the root causes of climate change, while adaptation focuses on building resilience to its unavoidable impacts. Integrating these strategies is crucial to combating climate change effectively and ensuring a sustainable future for all. Here, we explore key mitigation and adaptation strategies that pave the way for a resilient and low-carbon future.

a). Transition to Renewable Energy and Energy Efficiency Improvements.

Shifting from fossil fuels to renewable sources like solar, wind, and hydroelectric power reduces emissions, fostering a cleaner energy landscape. Enhancing energy efficiency in industries, buildings, and transportation reduces energy consumption, curbing emissions and lowering operational costs.

c). Reforestation and Afforestation and of Sustainable Agriculture

Planting trees and restoring forests absorb CO_2, acting as natural carbon sinks, mitigating climate change and preserving biodiversity. Encouraging sustainable farming practices, agroforestry, and soil conservation minimizes emissions from agriculture and promotes carbon sequestration.

e). Carbon Pricing and Taxation:-Implementing carbon pricing mechanisms like carbon taxes or cap-and-trade systems incentivizes businesses to reduce emissions and invest in cleaner technologies.

3.18.ENERGY ISSUES IN SUSTAINABLE DEVELOPMENT

A. Transitioning to Renewable Energy Sources

The transitions to renewable energy sources stands at the forefront of the global efforts to combat climate change and foster a sustainable future. Embracing renewable energy technologies not only reduces greenhouse gas emissions but also promotes energy independence, creates jobs, and drives innovation., the key aspects of transitioning to renewable energy sources and the transformative impact it has on societies and the environment include the following.

B.) Harnessing Solar Energy:

Solar Photovoltaic (PV) Systems convert sunlight into electricity, providing a clean and abundant source of energy. Advances in solar technology enhance efficiency and affordability, making solar power accessible to a broader range of consumers. Concentrated Solar Power (CSP)systems use mirrors or lenses to concentrate sunlight onto a small area, generating high-temperature heat that drives turbines, producing electricity. CSP is particularly effective in areas with abundant sunlight and contributes to grid stability.

C. LEVERAGING WIND POWER AND HYDROPOWER:

Onshore and Offshore Wind Farms wind farms harness the kinetic energy from the wind to generate electricity. Offshore wind farms, situated in coastal areas, benefit from consistent winds and contribute significantly to renewable energy capacity. Hydropower systems utilize flowing water to generate electricity without significant water storage. Pumped storage hydropower involves storing excess energy by pumping water uphill, releasing it later to generate electricity during peak demand.

D. Tapping into Biomass Energy/ Biogas and Biomass Power Plants: - Biogas, derived from organic waste, and biomass power plants, utilizing organic materials such as wood pellets, agricultural residues, and municipal solid waste, generate renewable energy while managing organic waste streams.

E. Exploring Geothermal Energy/Geothermal Power Plants: - Geothermal power plants utilize the Earth's natural heat from beneath the surface to generate electricity. This reliable and consistent source of energy is particularly prevalent in geologically active regions.

6. Fostering Innovation in Energy Storage: / Battery Technology: - Advances in battery technology enable the storage of surplus energy generated from renewables. Efficient energy storage solutions ensure a stable energy supply, even during periods of low renewable generation.

7. Promoting Smart Grids and Grid Modernization: - Smart grids integrate digital communication and control technologies, enabling real-time monitoring and management of energy distribution. This enhances grid efficiency, accommodates renewable energy variability, and reduces energy losses.

8. Investing in Research and Development/ Innovation and Collaboration: Continued investment in research and development fosters innovation in renewable energy technologies. Collaborative efforts between governments, academia, and the private sector drive advancements, making renewables more efficient, affordable, and widely accessible.

9. Promoting Energy Efficiency/ Energy Conservation: -Promoting energy efficiency in industries, buildings, and transportation sectors reduces overall energy demand. Combined with renewable energy sources, energy efficiency measures contribute significantly to mitigating climate change.

10. Communities Engagement

Educating communities about the benefits of renewable energy sources and involving them in the transition process fosters public support. Awareness campaigns and community engagement initiatives create a sense of ownership and commitment to sustainable energy practices. Transitioning to renewable energy sources represents a transformative shift toward a more sustainable and environmentally friendly energy landscape. By investing in renewable technologies, promoting energy efficiency, and fostering widespread public engagement, societies can accelerate this transition, reduce carbon emissions, and pave the way for a cleaner, greener future for generations to come.

3.19. ENERGY EFFICIENCY AND CONSERVATION MEASURES

Energy efficiency and conservation measures are crucial components of global efforts to mitigate climate change and ensure sustainable energy use. International agreements such as the Paris Agreement emphasize the significance of enhancing energy efficiency to reduce greenhouse gas emissions and promote sustainable development. These agreements encourage countries to implement energy-saving technologies, improve industrial processes, and enhance building standards to decrease energy consumption. By embracing energy efficiency and conservation measures outlined in international agreements, nations can reduce their carbon footprint, conserve valuable resources, and contribute to a more sustainable and environmentally friendly future for all.[228] Energy efficiency and conservation measures are fundamental pillars of sustainable energy practices, offering significant environmental, economic, and societal benefits. By optimizing energy usage and reducing waste, societies can mitigate climate change, lower energy costs, enhance energy security, and promote a greener future. Here, we explore key energy efficiency and conservation measures that empower sustainable practices and contribute to a more resilient and sustainable world.

a). Industrial and Commercial Efficiency/ Energy Audits and Process Optimization. Conducting energy audits in industrial and commercial sectors identifies inefficiencies and wasteful practices. Optimizing manufacturing processes and equipment usage reduces energy consumption, enhancing productivity and profitability. Industrial and commercial efficiency play a vital role in sustainable energy management. Energy audits, essential tools for identifying energy wastage and inefficiencies, enable businesses to optimize their operations and reduce energy consumption significantly.[229]

b). Transportation Efficiency/ Public Transportation and Carpooling.

Efficient transportation systems, including well-developed public transportation networks, are essential for reducing traffic congestion and greenhouse gas emissions. Public transportation not only decreases individual vehicle usage but also promotes sustainable urban development and reduces air pollution, making cities more livable and eco-friendly. Encouraging the use of public transportation and carpooling reduces individual vehicle emissions. Investment in efficient public transit systems provides eco-friendly commuting alternatives.

d). Behavioral Changes and Education/ Energy Conservation Awareness.

Educating individuals and communities about energy conservation practices raises awareness. Promoting behaviors like turning off lights when not in use, unplugging electronics, and reducing water heating temperatures instills energy-conscious habits.

---

[228] United Nations Framework Convention on Climate Change (UNFCCC). (2015). Paris Agreement. Retrieved from https://unfccc.int/process/the-paris-agreement/the-paris-agreement

[229] U.S. Department of Energy. Energy Audits & Assessments. https://www.iea.org/ Reports/energy -efficiency-2021

e). Government Incentives and Policies/ Energy Efficiency Standards.

Implementing and enforcing energy efficiency standards for appliances, buildings, and vehicles incentivizes manufacturers and consumers to adopt energy-efficient technologies.

F).ENERGY MANAGEMENT SYSTEMS/ BUILDING AUTOMATION SYSTEMS (BAS)

BAS monitor and control building systems, optimizing energy usage. Automated lighting, HVAC, and occupancy sensors adjust energy consumption based on real-time data, enhancing efficiency. Embracing energy efficiency and conservation measures is essential in the transition toward a sustainable energy future. By integrating these practices into daily lives, industries, and policies, societies can significantly reduce energy consumption, minimize environmental impact, and pave the way for a more energy-efficient, cost-effective, and environmentally friendly world.

3.20. BALANCING ENERGY NEEDS WITH ENVIRONMENTAL SUSTAINABILITY

1. Sustainable Management of Water Resources

Sustainable management of water resources is vital for ensuring the well-being of both people and the planet. This approach involves balancing the water needs of present and future generations while safeguarding the ecological integrity of aquatic ecosystems. Conservation efforts focus on reducing water wastage through efficient irrigation methods, promoting water-saving technologies in industries, and encouraging responsible domestic water usage. Additionally, sustainable management incorporates the protection and restoration of watersheds, wetlands, and aquatic habitats. By safeguarding these natural ecosystems, societies enhance water quality, preserve biodiversity, and promote resilience against droughts and floods.

Moreover, sustainable water management emphasizes equitable access to clean and safe water for all communities, addressing issues of social justice and equality. This approach involves ensuring that vulnerable populations, including marginalized communities and those in arid regions, have access to reliable water sources. Education and awareness campaigns play a crucial role, informing people about the value of water, promoting conservation habits, and fostering a sense of responsibility toward the environment. By integrating these strategies, societies can ensure the sustainable availability of water resources, fostering a harmonious balance between human needs, ecological requirements, and the preservation of this precious natural resource for future generations.

2.RESPONSIBLE LAND USE PLANNING AND CONSERVATION

Responsible land use planning and conservation are integral components of sustainable development, emphasizing the judicious utilization and preservation of land resources. Effective land use planning involves assessing the environmental, social, and economic aspects of an area to make informed decisions about development activities. Conservation efforts focus on preserving natural habitats, biodiversity, and cultural heritage sites. This approach ensures that development projects do not encroach upon ecologically sensitive areas, maintaining the balance between human needs and environmental preservation. Responsible land use planning also promotes smart urbanization, encouraging compact and sustainable cities, reducing urban sprawl, and preserving agricultural land and green spaces.

3.CIRCULAR ECONOMY AND WASTE MANAGEMENT

the circular economy and waste management are crucial elements of sustainable development, emphasizing the shift from a linear "take-make-dispose" model to a more circular approach where resources are reused, recycled, and repurposed. In a circular economy, products, materials, and resources are kept in use for as long as possible, minimizing waste generation and reducing environmental impact. Waste management within this framework focuses on responsible disposal, recycling, and the recovery of valuable resources from waste materials. Circular economy principles encourage product design that considers recyclability and longevity, encouraging manufacturers to create items with minimal environmental impact. Additionally, waste management strategies, such as source segregation, recycling facilities, and composting initiatives, help divert waste from landfills, conserving valuable resources and reducing pollution.

3.21. CHALLENGES AND BARRIERS TO SUSTAINABLE DEVELOPMENT

A sustainable development, while crucial for the well-being of current and future generations, faces a multitude of challenges and barriers that hinder its progress. This paper explores three major categories of obstacles to sustainable development: economic and political challenges, technological limitations, and issues related to public awareness and education.

1.ECONOMIC AND POLITICAL CHALLENGES

Economic and political challenges present significant hurdles to sustainable development efforts. In many cases, short-term economic interests conflict with long-term sustainability goals. Industries reliant on non-renewable resources often resist transitioning to sustainable practices due to economic concerns, fearing increased costs and reduced competitiveness. Additionally, political instability and corruption can impede the formulation and implementation of sustainable policies. Political leaders may prioritize immediate economic gains over environmental conservation and social equity, leading to unsustainable resource exploitation and environmental degradation.

2.TECHNOLOGICAL LIMITATIONS

Technological limitations pose a significant barrier to achieving sustainable development goals. While advancements in renewable energy, water purification, and waste management have been made, there remain gaps in technology adoption, especially in developing regions. Limited access to affordable and efficient sustainable technologies hampers progress. Additionally, the development and deployment of new, innovative solutions require substantial research and investment. In some cases, the lack of technical expertise and infrastructure prevents the implementation of sustainable technologies

3.PUBLIC AWARENESS AND EDUCATION

Public awareness and education play a crucial role in sustainable development. Lack of awareness and understanding of environmental issues, climate change, and sustainable practices often result in apathy and indifference. Inadequate environmental education in schools and communities further perpetuates this problem. Moreover, misinformation and greenwashing (misleading information about a product's environmental impact) can misguide consumers and businesses, hindering their ability to make informed, sustainable choices.

CHAPTER FOUR

EXPLORING THE INTERCONNECTED CHALLENGES OF ENVIRONMENTAL, SOCIAL, AND ECONOMIC JUSTICE IN THE PURSUIT OF GLOBAL EQUITY.

4.01. Introduction to Environmental Justice

Environmental justice represents the history and continuing struggle of ordinary people for their civil, spatial, and human rights as members of a global ecological community.[230] Environmental justice entails equitable treatment and meaningful engagement of all individuals, irrespective of their race, color, national origin, or income, in the formulation, implementation, and enforcement of environmental laws, regulations, and policies. Equitable treatment implies that no community bears an undue burden of adverse environmental impacts arising from industrial, municipal, and commercial activities or the application of federal, state, and local laws, regulations, and policies. Environmental justice challenges discrimination and disparities in the allocation of the benefits and burdens of economic development. It fights against the discriminatory practices of dumping hazardous waste and toxic chemicals and placing waste disposals, incinerators, depots, and transportation routes in communities inhabited by people of color and poor people.[231] Meaningful involvement necessitates providing all communities with effective access to decision-makers and empowering them to make informed choices and positive contributions towards achieving environmental justice for themselves.[232]

4.02. Interconnectedness of Social Economic, and Environmental Disparities Environmental justice is a critical movement that addresses the intersection of social, economic, and environmental disparities, aiming to ensure that all communities, regardless of race, income, or social status, have the same degree of protection from environmental and health hazards. This concept recognizes that marginalized and low-income communities often bear the brunt of environmental pollution, hazardous waste sites, and other ecological threats, leading to adverse health effects and reduced quality of life. Environmental justice advocates work towards fair

---

[230] Steady, Filomina Chioma, editor. *Environmental Justice in the New Millennium: Global Perspectives on Race, Ethnicity, and Human Rights*, page 4.
[231] Ibidem
[232] U.S. Department of Energy. "What is Environmental Justice?" Office of Legacy Management, U.S. Department of Energy, Retrieved from https://www.energy.gov/lm/what-environmental-justice#:~:text=Environmental%20justice%20is%20the%20fair,laws%2C%20regulations%2C%20and%20policies.

treatment and meaningful involvement of all people in the development, implementation, and enforcement of environmental laws, regulations, and policies.

By promoting equality and inclusivity in environmental decision-making processes, environmental justice seeks to rectify historical injustices and create a sustainable future where every individual can live in a healthy environment, irrespective of their background or location as environmental challenges have also been rooted in the historical legacy of conservation initiatives, which involved the appropriation of African lands for game reserves. These reserves, marked by racial segregation, prohibited Africans from accessing them. The conservation efforts focused on utilizing and safeguarding wild animals for purposes such as conservation itself, sport, and recreation, creating a dichotomy where black communities were excluded.[233]

4.03.EQUITABLE ENVIRONMENTAL POLICIES AND PRACTICES

In recent decades, the environmental justice movement has gained momentum globally, emphasizing the need for equitable environmental policies and practices. Environmental justice recognizes the interconnectedness of social and environmental issues, emphasizing the importance of empowering communities to advocate for their rights to a clean and healthy environment. This movement challenges systemic inequalities, advocating for policies that address the disproportionate environmental burdens faced by marginalized communities. Moreover, environmental justice initiatives emphasize the significance of community engagement, education, and collaboration to foster sustainable solutions that uplift vulnerable populations. As societies continue to grapple with environmental challenges, the principles of environmental justice remain pivotal in shaping policies and fostering a more equitable and sustainable future for all. Environmental sustainability can only be achieved in the context of fair, effective and transparent national governance arrangements and the rule of law predicated on public participation in decision-making, access to justice and information, in accordance with Principle 10 of the Rio Declaration, exploring the potential value of borrowing provisions from the Aarhus Convention. In this regard, accessible, fair, impartial, timely, and responsive dispute resolution mechanisms, including developing specialized expertise in environmental adjudication, and innovative environmental procedures and remedies, recognition of the relationship between human rights and

---

[233] Steady, Filomina Chioma, editor. *Environmental Justice in the New Millennium: Global Perspectives on Race, Ethnicity, and Human Rights,* page 9.

the environment, and specific criteria for the interpretation of environmental law are important considerations.[234]

4.04. The Global Historical Context of Environmental Injustice.

Environmental justice is a social movement that emerged in the United States during the 1980s in response to the unequal environmental burdens experienced by marginalized communities, particularly low-income communities and people of color. The movement was a response to the environmental racism prevalent in many parts of the country, where hazardous waste sites, landfills, and polluting industries were disproportionately located in minority neighborhoods.[235] The concept of environmental justice highlighted the link between environmental degradation and social injustice, emphasizing that minority and low-income communities often bore the brunt of environmental pollution and its associated health risks. The environmental justice movement has articulated distinct objectives centered on eradicating the disproportionate enforcement of laws related to the environment, civil rights, housing, transportation, facility siting, and public health. Communities are actively engaged in efforts to eliminate their exposure to hazardous chemicals, pesticides, and other toxins within their homes, schools, neighborhoods, and workplaces. They are actively challenging the validity of the scientific processes and flawed assumptions guiding the selection of sites for polluting facilities, as well as the assessment, calculation, and management of associated risks. In numerous instances, the only discernible "science" influencing the placement of locally unwanted land uses, is essentially political science.[236] This movement gained momentum in the 1980s and 1990s, with activists and scholars advocating for fair treatment and involvement of all people in the development, implementation, and enforcement of environmental laws, regulations, and policies.[237]Over time, the environmental justice movement expanded beyond the United States and became a global phenomenon, with activists addressing environmental inequalities in various countries and advocating for the rights of vulnerable communities. The movement also influenced policies and led to the establishment of

---

[234] UNEP. "Environmental Rule of Law." http://www.unep.org/delc/worldcongress/ Home/tabid/55710/ Default.aspx. Part II, 3rd

[235] Bullard, Robert D. *Dumping in Dixie: Race, Class, and Environmental Quality.* Westview Press, 1990.

[236] Johnson, Glenn S. *Environmental Justice: A Brief History and Overview,* page 17.

[237] Mohai, Paul, David Pellow, and J. Timmons Roberts. "Environmental Justice." *Annual Review of Environment and Resources,* vol. 34, 2009, pp. 405-430.

environmental justice principles in decision-making processes, aiming to create a more equitable and sustainable future for all.[238]

4.05. An Overview of Environmental Injustices in Africa.

1. South Africa

South Africa, a nation where race has long played a significant role in societal organization, has been contending with various aspects of environmental justice and environmental racism.[239] The two prominent environmental justice issues facing South Africa are international dumping and nuclear energy. Despite formal changes, apartheid's enduring impact is evident in de facto terms, manifested through racial disparities, residential segregation, and the disposal of hazardous waste and toxic chemicals in areas predominantly inhabited by Africans. Furthermore, nuclear energy programs impose uneven burdens and risks, particularly disadvantaging African communities.[240] Environmental challenges are also rooted in the historical legacy of conservation initiatives, which involved the appropriation of African lands for game reserves. These reserves, marked by racial segregation, prohibited Africans from accessing them. The conservation efforts focused on utilizing and safeguarding wild animals for purposes such as conservation itself, sport, and recreation, creating a dichotomy where black communities were excluded.[241]

2. ENVIRONMENTAL INJUSTICES IN KENYA

- **Challenges Faced by The Urban Poor- KM & 9 others v Attorney General & 7 others.** Residents of Owino-Uhuru Village in Mombasa County, Kenya, sued through a petition alleging that a neighboring lead acid battery recycling factory, established on a plot leased by a private party, had caused severe environmental and health issues. The densely populated village, existing since the 1930s and 40s on about 13.5 acres of land, experienced toxic waste leakage from the factory. This contamination has led to numerous illnesses and ailments among the residents, with over 20 deaths attributed to lead poisoning.[242] The petition sought redress for the environmental injustices and health hazards inflicted upon the community. The Owino Uhuru slums case in Kenya exemplifies pervasive environmental injustices disproportionately affecting impoverished communities and has become a poignant symbol of the challenges faced by the urban poor. The

---

[238] Schlosberg, D. (2004). Reconceiving environmental justice: Global movements and political theories. Environmental Politics, 13(3), 517-540.

[239] McDonald, David, editor. "Introduction." *Environmental Justice in South Africa.*

[240] Ibidem

[241] Ibidem

[242] KM & 9 others v Attorney General & 7 others [2020] eKLR

slum's residents endured severe environmental hazards, including inadequate waste management, limited access to clean water, and substandard sanitation facilities. These deficiencies in basic services perpetuate a cycle of health issues and economic hardship, highlighting the systemic neglect of marginalized populations in Kenya. The environmental injustices in Owino Uhuru underscore a broader pattern of neglect and discrimination faced by low-income communities across the country. Factors such as inadequate urban planning, government inaction, and a lack of infrastructure investment contribute to the dire living conditions in these slums. Residents bear the brunt of environmental hazards, leading to a range of health problems and hindering their ability to break free from the cycle of poverty. The case serves as a stark reminder of the urgent need for comprehensive and equitable environmental policies that prioritize the well-being of all citizens, regardless of socio-economic status.

•CHALLENGES FACED BY THE INDIGENOUS COMMUNITIES

In Kenya, the Mau Forest serves as the ancestral homeland for the Ogiek people, an indigenous community numbering 20,000 individuals, with approximately 15,000 residing within the expansive Mau Forest Complex spanning approximately 400,000 hectares. Organized into clans, the Ogiek maintain distinct linguistic and societal practices, relying on the Mau Forest for centuries as both their habitat and primary means of sustenance. As a hunter-gatherer community, the Ogiek have intricately woven their lives with the resources provided by the Mau Forest, establishing a deep-rooted connection to the land.[243] The Ogiek approached the Kenyan courts seeking redress and a declaration that the right to life protection by section 71 of the previous Constitution of every member of the Ogiek Community in Mau Forest including the Applicants has been contravened, by forcible eviction from their parcels of land in the Mau Forest.[244] The Ogiek pursued legal avenues to defend their land rights. to the African Court on Human and Peoples' Rights, with the Ogiek arguing that the government's actions violated their rights to property, culture, and a healthy environment. The court's decisions were crucial in addressing not only the Ogiek case but also broader issues of indigenous land rights and environmental justice. The case highlighted the impact of environmental injustices on indigenous and marginalized communities.

[243]Amnesty International. "Ogiek Case: Protection of an Indigenous Community in Kenya." Amnesty

International, 2023, https://www.amnesty.org/en/
latest/campaigns/2023/06/ogiek-case- protection-
of-an-indigenous-community-in-kenya/
#:~:text=After%20years%20of%20struggle%
20with,cultural%20specificities%20must%20be
%20protected.
[244] Joseph Letuya & 21 others v Attorney General & 5 others
[2014] eKLR

4.06.IMPACT OF ENVIRONMENTAL INJUSTICES ON INDIGENOUS COMMUNITIES IN KENYA:

a) **Displacement and Loss of Livelihoods:** Indigenous communities like the Ogiek often rely on specific ecosystems for their traditional livelihoods. Environmental injustices, such as forced evictions or restrictions on land use, can result in displacement and the loss of vital resources, disrupting their traditional ways of life.

b) **Cultural Erosion:** Indigenous cultures are deeply intertwined with their natural surroundings. Environmental injustices, including the degradation of ancestral lands, threaten indigenous cultures as they lose access to sacred sites, traditional practices, and the knowledge passed down through generations.

c) **Limited Access to Resources:** Indigenous communities often depend on local ecosystems for resources like food, medicine, and building materials. Environmental degradation, whether due to government policies or external factors, limits their access to these resources, impacting their health and overall well-being.

d) **Marginalization and Discrimination:** Environmental policies that disproportionately affect indigenous communities contribute to their marginalization. Discriminatory practices, such as denying land rights or excluding them from decision-making processes, exacerbate social and economic disparities, further disenfranchising these communities.

e) **Loss of Biodiversity and Ecological Knowledge:** Indigenous communities often possess valuable knowledge about local ecosystems and sustainable resource management. Environmental injustices that undermine their connection to the land result in the loss of this ecological knowledge, hindering broader conservation efforts and sustainable development.

4.07 THE EVOLUTION AND STATUS OF ENVIRONMENTAL JUSTICE IN KENYA

Environmental justice in Kenya has a complex historical context, with significant developments occurring after the promulgation of the new constitution in 2010. Before the constitution, Kenya faced numerous environmental challenges, including deforestation, pollution, land degradation, and loss of biodiversity. These issues disproportionately affected marginalized communities, leading to environmental injustices. The court has held that Litigation aimed at protecting the environment in Kenya, cannot be shackled by the narrow application of the *locus standi rule*, both under the Constitution and statute, and indeed in principle. Any person, without the need of demonstrating personal injury, has the freedom and capacity to institute an action aimed at protecting the environment.[245] The judiciary has underscored the significance of these rights, highlighting their acknowledgment of the critical connection between a clean and secure environment and economic and social rights. This acknowledgment stems from the understanding that the environment significantly influences an individual's quality of life and safety.[246] As has been rightly observed by Alexander Kiss, "an environment degraded by pollution and defaced by the destruction of all beauty and variety is as contrary to satisfactory living conditions and the development as the breakdown of the fundamental ecologic equilibria is harmful to physical and moral health."

B.) The 2010 Kenyan Constitution

he advent of the 2010 Kenyan Constitution signaled a pivotal moment for environmental justice within the nation. This constitutional milestone acknowledged the right to a clean and healthy environment as a fundamental human right. Specifically, Article 42 explicitly declares that every individual possesses the right to a clean and healthy environment, encompassing the entitlement to environmental protection for the well-being of both current and future generations.[247]

• ARTICLE 22(1) OF THE CONSTITUTION

Article 22(1) of the Constitution ensures a crucial avenue for individuals to safeguard their rights, including those pertaining to the environment, through legal means. This constitutional provision guarantees every person the right to initiate court proceedings, asserting that a right or fundamental freedom enshrined in the Bill of Rights has been denied, violated, infringed upon, or is under threat. Consequently, this empowers individuals to seek legal recourse to prevent or address violations or threats to their environmental rights through litigation.[248]

•ARTICLE 42 OF THE CONSTITUTION

If an individual contends that their right to a clean and healthy environment, as acknowledged and safeguarded under Article 42, is being, has been, or is likely to be denied, violated, infringed, or threatened, they have the right to seek redress through legal channels. This includes the option to apply to a court for remedies, in addition to any other available legal avenues for the same issue. Importantly, under this Article, the applicant is not obligated to demonstrate that any person has

---

[245] Joseph Leboo & 2 others v Director Kenya Forest Services & another

[246] Martin Osano Rabera & Another vs. Municipal Council of Nakuru & 2 others [2018] eKLR

[247] Constitution of Kenya, 2010, Article 42.

[248] Constitution of Kenya, 2010, Article 22(1).

incurred loss or suffered injury for the application to be considered valid. The focus is on the potential or actual infringement of the right to a clean and healthy environment.[249]

•ARTICLE 70(1) OF THE CONSTITUTION

Indeed, the Constitution extends its provisions by specifying that, upon such an application, the court is empowered to issue any order or directions it deems fitting. These orders may include actions to prevent, stop, or discontinue any harmful act or omission affecting the environment. Furthermore, the court may compel public officers to take necessary measures to prevent or discontinue activities detrimental to the environment. Additionally, the court is authorized to grant compensation to any victim whose right to a clean and healthy environment has been violated. This reinforces the constitutional commitment to ensuring the protection and enforcement of environmental rights through legal measures.[250] In the years following the adoption of the new constitution, there have been significant efforts to address environmental injustices in Kenya. The government, along with non-governmental organizations and grassroots movements, has worked to enforce environmental laws and regulations more effectively. This has led to increased accountability for industries and individuals that pollute or harm the environment. Community participation in environmental decision-making processes has also improved. Local communities, especially indigenous peoples, have gained recognition and legal protection for their traditional knowledge and practices related to environmental conservation. This acknowledgment has helped in the preservation of natural resources and biodiversity.

C.) Environmental Issues and Social Justice

Additionally, there has been a growing awareness of the link between environmental issues and social justice in Kenya. Environmental justice movements have gained momentum, advocating for the rights of communities affected by large-scale development projects, land grabbing, and environmental degradation. These movements have played a crucial role in raising awareness about environmental injustices and holding both public and private entities accountable for their actions. Despite these positive developments, challenges remain. Enforcement of environmental laws can be inconsistent, and marginalized communities still face obstacles in accessing justice. Additionally, the impacts of climate change continue to pose significant challenges to environmental sustainability and justice in the country.

[249] Constitution of Kenya, 2010, Article 42

[250] Constitution of Kenya, 2010, Article 70(1).

The period post the 2010 Kenyan Constitution has seen important strides in recognizing and addressing environmental injustices. The constitution itself provided a strong legal foundation for environmental protection and the promotion of environmental justice. Ongoing efforts by the government, civil society, and grassroots movements are crucial in ensuring that these principles are upheld and that all Kenyan citizens can enjoy a clean and healthy environment.

4.04. The Fundamental Elements of Environmental Justice.

Environmental justice is a critical framework that addresses the unequal distribution of environmental benefits and burdens among communities, emphasizing the fair treatment of all individuals regardless of their socioeconomic status, race, or ethnicity. At its core, environmental justice advocates for equitable access to a clean and healthy environment and asserts that no community should bear a disproportionate share of environmental pollution or hazards. This concept encompasses several fundamental principles and tenets. It champions equity and fairness, striving to eliminate disparities in environmental risks and ensuring that marginalized populations are not unfairly burdened by environmental challenges. Additionally, environmental justice promotes community participation, transparency, and accountability, fostering inclusive decision- making processes and holding both public and private entities responsible for their environmental actions. These principles guide efforts to create a more just and sustainable environment for all, reflecting a vision where every individual and community can thrive in a healthy living environment.

A. THE BASIC PRINCIPLES AND TENETS OF ENVIRONMENTAL JUSTICE INCLUDE:

1. **Equity and Fairness:** Environmental justice emphasizes the fair and equal treatment of all individuals, regardless of their race, ethnicity, socioeconomic status, or location. It advocates for the elimination of disparities in the distribution of environmental benefits and burdens, ensuring that marginalized communities are not disproportionately affected by environmental hazards [251]

2. **Community Participation:** Environmental justice promotes inclusive decision-making processes that involve local communities, especially those historically excluded or underrepresented. It recognizes the importance of meaningful public participation in environmental policy-making, planning, and implementation, allowing communities to voice their concerns and contribute to shaping their local environments[252]

[251] Bullard, R. D. (1990). Dumping in Dixie: Race, Class, and Environmental Quality. Westview Press.
[252] Schlosberg, D. (2004). Reconceiving Environmental Justice: Global Movements and Political

3. Accountability and Transparency: The principle of accountability holds both public and private entities responsible for their environmental actions. Environmental justice demands transparent and accessible information about environmental policies, projects, and potential hazards. It also calls for accountability mechanisms, ensuring that violators of environmental regulations are held responsible and face appropriate consequences.[253]

4. Precautionary Approach: Environmental justice advocates for the application of the precautionary principle, urging decision-makers to take preventive action in the face of uncertainty. This principle implies that if an action, policy, or project has the potential to cause harm to the public or the environment, in the absence of scientific consensus, the burden of proof falls on those advocating for the action, rather than those opposing it.[254]

5. Environmental Sustainability: Environmental justice recognizes the interdependence of social, economic, and environmental factors. It promotes sustainable development practices that meet the needs of the present without compromising the ability of future generations to meet their own needs. This involves preserving natural resources, conserving biodiversity, and mitigating climate change impacts (United Nations, 1992).[255]

4.09. The pillars of environmental justice

The 1998 Aarhus Convention on Access to Information, Public Participation in Decision-Making and Access to Justice in Environmental Matters, the UN Environment's 2010 Guidelines for the Development of National Legislation on Access to Information, Public Participation and Access to Justice in Environmental Matters (Bali Guidelines) form comprehensive international environmental law instruments provided international standards of best practice for countries' environmental governance. These instruments gave rise to the 3 environmental "Access Rights"

i.e. people's rights of access to information, access to public participation and access to justice in environmental matters – now considered the "3 Pillars" of the environmental rule of law.[256]

Theories. Environmental Politics, 13(3), 517-540.

[253] Mohai, P., Pellow, D., & Roberts, J. T. (2009). Environmental Justice. Annual Review of Environment and Resources, 34, 405-430.

[254] Nanda, V., & Pring, G. (2013). International Environmental Law and Policy for the 21st Century (2nd rev. ed.). Aspen Publishers.

[255] United Nations. (1992). Rio Declaration on Environment and Development. United Nations Conference on Environment & Development.

[256] Pring, G., & Pring, C. (2009). Greening Justice: Creating and Improving Environmental Courts and Tribunals (pp. 6-9). Retrieved from http://www.law.du.edu/ect-study.

A.) Access Rights to Information in Environmental Matters:

Access rights, concerning people's rights to information regarding environmental matters, are fundamental in fostering transparency, public participation, and accountability. International conventions such as the Aarhus Convention and Kenyan laws, including Article 35 of the Constitution, underline the significance of these rights. They empower citizens to access environmental information held by public authorities, promoting informed decision-making and active involvement in environmental governance.

1. **Aarhus Convention:** The Aarhus Convention, adopted in 1998, emphasizes public participation in environmental decision-making processes. It grants individuals and communities the right to access environmental information, participate in environmental impact assessment procedures, and challenge decisions that affect the environment. This international agreement has significantly influenced national legislations worldwide, including Kenya's policies on access to environmental information.[257]

2. **Kenyan Constitution** - Article 35 of the Kenyan Constitution guarantees the right to access information held by the State. It stipulates that every citizen has the right to access any information held by the State or any other entity that is required for the exercise or protection of any right or fundamental freedom. This constitutional provision underscores the importance of access to information in upholding citizens' rights and promoting transparency in governmental actions.[258]

3. **Judicial Precedents:** Judicial precedents,

from courts in Kenya, have reinforced the significance of access rights. Landmark cases have clarified the scope and application of these rights, ensuring that citizens have the legal standing to challenge environmental decisions that impact their communities. These judgments have contributed to the jurisprudence on access to environmental information and have shaped the legal landscape in Kenya.[259] Kenyan courts, have consistently upheld access rights, affirming citizens' entitlement to environmental information. The court emphasized that access to information stands as a fundamental pillar within our constitutional framework for environmental governance. It underscored that effective public

[257] United Nations Economic Commission for Europe (UNECE). (1998). *Convention on Access to Information, Public Participation in Decision-Making and Access to Justice in Environmental Matters* (Aarhus Convention). Retrieved from_http://www.unece. org/env/pp/ documents /ce p 43e.pdf

[258] Constitution of Kenya. (2010). Retrieved from http://www.kenyalaw.org:8181/exist/kenyalex/ actview.xql?actid=Const2010.

[259]*Matters* (Aarhus Convention). Retrieved from http://www.unece.org/env/pp/ documents/ cep43e.pdf.

participation in decision-making processes relies significantly on complete, accurate, and timely information. Furthermore, the court delineated two fundamental aspects of the right to access information in environmental matters, the "*passive*" aspect encompasses the public's right to request information from public authorities, coupled with the obligation of these authorities to furnish the requested information upon inquiry and the "*active*" aspect entails the public's entitlement to receive information without a specific request and the corresponding duty of authorities to proactively collect and disseminate information of public interest. This obligation exists irrespective of whether a specific inquiry has been made, ensuring continuous transparency and accessibility of relevant information to the public.[260] In the case of *Mohamed Ali Baadi and others v Attorney General & 11 others [2018] eKLR*, the High Court emphasized the importance of access rights, stating that the public's right to information in environmental matters is essential for informed decision-making. The right to access information is fundamental, allowing individuals to obtain information held by public authorities.[261] Additionally, in the case of *Katiba Institute V Presidents Delivery Unit & 3 others [2017] eKLR*), the court underscored that access to information is a fundamental right, and public authorities must provide relevant environmental information promptly upon request. This right is essential for transparent and democratic governance, enabling citizens to actively participate in their government's affairs. Effective public participation hinges on citizens' ability to access information held by public authorities; without this knowledge, meaningful engagement in governance is compromised. The right to access information forms the bedrock of other rights, ensuring citizens can protect and exercise their democratic freedoms. This right is crucial for fostering an informed and engaged citizenry, pivotal in upholding the principles of democracy.[262]

4. **Environmental Management and Coordination Act (EMCA):** EMCA, the primary environmental law in Kenya, incorporates provisions related to access to environmental information. Section 29 of EMCA grants the public the right to access environmental information held by any public institution. It outlines the procedure for requesting information and imposes obligations on public authorities to provide such information, aligning with international standards and the constitutional mandate for access rights.[263]

---

[260] Mohamed Ali Baadi and others v Attorney General & 11 Others [2018] eKLR

[261] Ibid

[262] Katiba Institute V Presidents Delivery Unit & 3 others [2017] eKLR

[263] Sec 29 of the Environmental Management and Coordination Act. (1999). Retrieved from http://extwprlegs1.fao.org/docs/pdf/ken54647.pdf

5. ROLE OF CIVIL SOCIETY IN PROMOTING ACCESS TO INFORMATION

Civil society organizations play a significant role in advocating for access rights in Kenya. Through research, legal interventions, and awareness campaigns, the organization promotes transparency and accountability in environmental governance. Their efforts focus on ensuring that citizens can obtain relevant information, empowering them to actively participate in decisions affecting their environment. International conventions, constitutional provisions, judicial decisions, and civil society initiatives collectively underscore the importance of access rights in environmental matters, enabling citizens to play an active role in environmental protection and sustainable development.

B.) Access to Public Participation in Environmental Matters.

1. Right to public participation in environmental matters

International conventions such as the Aarhus Convention form the foundation for the right to public participation in environmental matters. The Aarhus Convention, ratified by Kenya, recognizes the importance of public participation in decision-making processes related to the environment. It establishes the right of citizens to participate in environmental decision-making and grants them access to environmental information. This principle underscores the international commitment to fostering transparency and citizen involvement in environmental governance .[264] In *Constitutional Petition E053 of 2021,* the court affirmed that the principle of public participation was not a recent development and had always been an inherent component of the common law doctrine of natural justice. Both the Constitution and statutory laws had established the obligation of public participation across various aspects of governance. Denying public participation would contradict the constitutional mandate. The court emphasized that the respondents must consider the perspectives and values concerning environmental management held by communities likely to be impacted by decisions involving nearby or inhabited environmental resources, such as decisions on forest-related matters. These considerations were crucial in ensuring just and equitable environmental policies.[265]

---

[264] Aarhus Convention on Access to Information, Public Participation in Decision-making and Access to Justice in Environmental Matters (1998).

[265] Chega (Suing on their Own Behalf and as the Registered Official of Active Environment Team) v Kenya Forest Service & another; Kiambu Saw millers & 10 others (Interested Parties) (Constitutional Petition E053 of 2021) [2022] KEELC 13738 (KLR) (21 October 2022) (Judgment)

2. THE 2010 CONSTITUTION AND PUBLIC PARTICIPATION

In the Kenyan legal context, the 2010 Constitution guarantees the right to public participation under Article 10, emphasizing the importance of involving the public in environmental decision-making processes. In the case of *Mohamed Ali Baadi and others v Attorney General & 11 others [2018] eKLR*, the petitioners contested the conceptualization and execution of the LAPSSET Project, alleging violations of both constitutional and statutory laws. he petitioners raised objections to the project's design, asserting that it lacked sufficient measures to mitigate its adverse effects. Their primary argument was that the implementation of the Lamu Port, South Sudan, Ethiopia Transport Corridor (LAPSSET) Project disregarded fundamental principles and values, such as sustainable development, transparency, public participation, and accountability. Furthermore, they contended that the project's execution was violating their constitutional rights, including the right to earn a livelihood, a clean and healthy environment, cultural rights, and the right to information. In response, the Court determined and affirmed that the conceptualization and implementation of the LAPSSET Project were both unlawful and unconstitutional. The High Court, in its ruling, upheld the constitutional right to public participation, emphasizing that it serves as a cornerstone of democratic governance, particularly in environmental matters. This legal decision reinforces the importance of involving the public in decisions that may have significant environmental and social impacts, aligning with democratic principles and constitutional rights.[266]

3. CHALLENGES AND REMEDIES IN PUBLIC PARTICIPATION

Despite constitutional provisions, challenges persist in ensuring effective public participation.

a) **Limited Access to Information:** Lack of access to comprehensive and understandable information about environmental projects and their potential impacts hinders meaningful public participation. Incomplete or technical data can deter citizens from engaging in discussions effectively.

b) **Complexity of Environmental Issues:** Environmental matters often involve complex scientific, technical, and legal concepts. Understanding these complexities can be challenging for the general public, making it difficult for citizens to make informed contributions to discussions and decisions.

---

[266] Constitution of Kenya (2010), *Okiya Omtatah Okoiti v. Attorney General & 6 Others* (2013) [2013] eKLR.

c) **Inadequate Time and Resources:** Public consultation processes are sometimes conducted within tight timeframes, limiting the opportunity for citizens to thoroughly analyze proposals and provide meaningful feedback. Additionally, citizens may lack the necessary resources, such as time and funds, to actively participate in lengthy and resource-intensive consultation processes.

d) **Power Imbalance:** There might be a power imbalance between the public and the institutions or corporations involved in environmental decision-making. Communities, especially marginalized or vulnerable groups, may feel powerless in the face of powerful corporations or government agencies, discouraging them from participating openly.

e) **Limited Civic Education:** Insufficient education and awareness about environmental issues and the importance of citizen participation can hinder public engagement. Civic education programs are essential for empowering citizens to understand the relevance of their participation in environmental decision-making processes.

f) **Language and Cultural Barriers:** Language barriers and cultural differences can hinder effective communication between policymakers and the public, especially in multicultural societies. Certain communities might feel excluded or misunderstood due to language and cultural disparities, impacting their ability to participate meaningfully.

g) **Fragmented Participation:** Public participation efforts are sometimes fragmented and lack coordination. Different agencies or entities may conduct separate consultations on related issues, leading to disjointed input and limiting the holistic understanding of public concerns.

h) **Limited Influence on Decision-Making:** Public

input may not always translate into concrete changes in decision-making processes. If citizens perceive that their opinions do not influence outcomes, they may become disillusioned, leading to apathy and reduced future participation. Kenya, a nation rich in biodiversity and natural resources, has grappled with environmental challenges, leading to the establishment of specialized courts to address environmental disputes. These courts, governed by the Environment and Land Court Act, have been pivotal in shaping the jurisprudence surrounding environmental issues in Kenya. In recent years, Kenyan case law has provided crucial insights into the jurisdictional scope of these specialized courts, elucidating their role in safeguarding the country's environmental heritage.

4.10.LIABILITY IN ENVIRONMENTAL MATTERS.

Liability in environmental matters has become a pivotal focus in international agreements and conventions, acknowledging the urgent need to hold parties accountable for ecological damages. This concept revolves around attributing responsibility and seeking compensation for environmental harm caused by human activities. International agreements and conventions play a crucial role in shaping the framework of liability, ensuring that nations adhere to principles of environmental stewardship and sustainable development.[267]

1.) Shared Responsibility and Cross-Border Impact: One of the key aspects of liability in environmental matters pertains to shared responsibility. The Aarhus Convention, for instance, emphasizes public participation and access to justice in environmental decision-making processes. This ensures that not only states but also citizens and organizations are held accountable for their actions.

A.) Legislative Framework for Cross Border Environmental Liability.

The Basel Convention on the Control of Transboundary Movements of Hazardous Wastes and their Disposal, established in 1989 and enforced since 1992, stands as the preeminent international agreement concerning hazardous wastes and other wastes. This convention signifies a monumental stride in global environmental governance, addressing the critical challenges associated with the cross-border movement and disposal of hazardous materials. Uniting nations under a common cause, the Basel Convention sets stringent standards and protocols, ensuring the responsible management of hazardous wastes to safeguard both human health and the environment.

1.) **International** **Agreements** **and** **Conventions and the Framework for Liability:** Under the umbrella of international agreements such as the Stockholm Convention on Persistent Organic Pollutants and the Paris Agreement, nations are bound by specific protocols that address liability in environmental matters. These agreements emphasize the 'polluter pays' principle, wherein those responsible for environmental damage are financially liable. The International Court of Justice (ICJ) and the International Tribunal for the Law of the Sea (ITLOS) provide legal avenues for states to seek redress, ensuring accountability on the global stage.

2.) Shared responsibility among nations

In essence, the Basel Convention serves as a beacon of international cooperation, fostering shared responsibility among nations to prevent the adverse environmental and social impacts arising from

[267] United Nations Environment Programme. (2019). Basel Convention on the Control of Transboundary Movements of Hazardous Wastes and Their Disposal.

hazardous waste mismanagement. Its comprehensive framework encompasses a wide array of hazardous substances and materials, establishing a robust system for the identification, categorization, and regulation of these dangerous materials. By doing so, the convention curtails the unauthorized and harmful transboundary movements of hazardous wastes, promoting environmental sustainability and mitigating the risks posed to vulnerable communities and ecosystems. The Basel Convention on the Control of Transboundary Movements of Hazardous Wastes and Disposal emphasizes stringent regulations and principles of shared responsibility as a pivotal principle in shaping the global environmental agenda, promoting sustainable practices, and protecting the well-being of both humanity and the planet. It is conventions like the Basel Convention that provide the legal infrastructure that regulates the transboundary movements of hazardous wastes, preventing countries from dumping environmental burdens on others. This cooperative approach underscores the interconnectedness of environmental challenges and the necessity for collective responsibility.[268]

3. Equitable treatment of all nations and Ethical Disposal of Hazardous Wastes Furthermore, the Basel Convention underscores the principle of environmental justice, emphasizing the equitable treatment of all nations, regardless of their economic status. It promotes the ethical disposal of hazardous wastes, discouraging the export of such materials from developed to developing countries. This equitable approach ensures that the burden of hazardous waste management is shared globally, fostering a sense of solidarity and cooperation among nations. Despite the progress facilitated by international agreements, challenges in implementing liability frameworks persist. Variability in national legislation, lack of enforcement mechanisms, and evolving nature of environmental risks pose hurdles. Looking forward, strengthening the compliance mechanisms and ensuring stricter enforcement of liability provisions are essential. Furthermore, fostering international cooperation and encouraging states to ratify and implement agreements robustly will be crucial in addressing emerging environmental challenges effectively.

4.11. The Judicial Enforcement of Environmental Justice.

The judicial enforcement of environmental justice plays a pivotal role in ensuring that the principles of fairness, equity, and accountability are upheld in environmental matters. Courts serve as essential arenas where environmental justice claims are adjudicated, and rulings can significantly impact communities disproportionately affected by environmental issues. Through

[268] United Nations. (1998). The Basel Convention on the Control of Transboundary Movements of Hazardous Wastes.

legal proceedings, judges interpret and enforce environmental laws, holding both public and private entities accountable for their actions and ensuring that marginalized communities receive due protection. Judicial decisions can set crucial precedents, shaping environmental policies, regulations, and practices. Moreover, the judiciary's role extends beyond mere enforcement; it contributes to the development of a just and sustainable society by addressing environmental inequalities and fostering a sense of responsibility among stakeholders. As a result, the judicial enforcement of environmental justice stands as a cornerstone in the pursuit of a balanced and equitable environmental landscape.

The judiciary as an independent arm of the government bequeathed with the responsibility of interpreting the law, hearing, and determining disputes from different parties. The judiciary's position is self-evident as sacrosanct in matters of environmental justice and governance. This is especially important in improving the environmental rule of law, access to justice and environmental dispute resolution for achieving the country's goals of a healthy environment. These steps go a long way in protecting Kenya's heritage for future generations, in line with the United Nation's 2030 Agenda for Sustainable Development and the Sustainable Development Goals. The judiciary thus has a mandate to provides access to justice for all to build effective and accountable all-inclusive institutions at all levels.[269]

4.12. The need for special courts to deal with environmental matters. Environmental disputes involve a complex string of technical, scientific, and legal issues that require special expertise to solve, a special court with relevant expertise in environmental matters is therefore best placed to determine matters relating to environmental justice, in the achievement of ecologically sustainable development. These issues can range from environmental pollution and resource management to climate change impacts, involving complex data, regulations, and scientific knowledge. Given the complicated nature of these disputes, it is crucial to have specialized expertise to accurately interpret the evidence, assess the environmental impact, and understand the legal implications involved. Environmental justice, therefore, requires a specialized court that possesses the necessary proficiency in environmental matters to ensure fair and informed decisions.

---

[269] Pring, G. R., & Pring, C. (Year of publication). *A Guide for Policy Makers.* Global Environmental Outcomes LLC (GEO) and University of Denver Environmental Courts & Tribunals Study for the United Nations Environment Programme.

A) Role of specialized courts towards achieving environmental justice

Establishing specialized courts with expertise in environmental matters holds significant advantages. Such a court would consist of judges, legal experts, and professionals with deep understanding and experience in environmental sciences and regulations. This specialized knowledge equips the court to comprehensively evaluate evidence, assess environmental risks, and interpret complex laws and regulations related to environmental protection. Moreover, a dedicated environmental court can facilitate efficient and expedited proceedings, ensuring that cases are handled by professionals who are well-versed in the intricacies of environmental issues.

B.) Role of specialized courts towards achieving sustainable development

By entrusting environmental justice to a specialized court, societies can work towards achieving ecologically sustainable development. Such a court can contribute significantly to the protection of natural resources, biodiversity, and the overall environment. Through well-informed judgments and decisions, the court can set precedents that promote environmentally responsible practices and policies. In this way, the specialized court becomes a pivotal instrument in steering societies toward a more sustainable future, balancing the needs of development with the imperative of preserving the environment for future generations.

4.13. Legal framework for Environmental courts in Kenya A.) Article 162 of the constitution.

Environmental courts, established under Article 162

of the constitution, hold a distinct status as special courts. These courts are deemed superior, endowed with powers and authority equivalent to those of the standard High courts. Their jurisdiction is specifically tailored to encompass the hearing and resolution of disputes pertaining to environmental matters, as well as issues related to the use, occupation, and title of land. This designation emphasizes the significance placed on addressing environmental concerns and land-related disputes within a specialized legal framework, reinforcing the importance of these issues in the legal system.[270]

B.) Jurisdiction of Environmental Courts in Kenya.

Parliament has fulfilled its constitutional duty by enacting legislation that defines the jurisdiction of the Environment and Land Court. This specialized court holds both original and appellate jurisdiction, as stipulated in Article 162(2)(b) of the Constitution, to adjudicate all disputes pertaining to the environment and land in Kenya. The court's authority is not only derived from

---

[270] Article 162 (2) of The Constitution of Kenya 2010.

the constitutional provisions but is also explicitly outlined in Section 13 of the Environment and Land Court Act (ELC Act).

From an analysis of both the Constitution and the relevant Acts of Parliament, it is evident that a unique category of courts, possessing sui generis jurisdiction, has been established. The jurisdiction of this court is tied to the mandates articulated in Article 162(2)(b) of the Constitution and Section 13 of the Environment and Land Court Act, reinforcing its specialized role in handling legal matters concerning the environment and land in Kenya.[271]

1. **The status of the High Court to hear and determine disputes relating to the environment**

Article 162(2)(b) of the Constitution provides that Parliament shall establish courts with the status of the High Court to hear and determine disputes relating to the environment and the use and occupation of, and title to, land.[272] Parliament enacted the Environment and Land Court Act in compliance with the provisions of Article 162(3). Section 13 of the Environment and Land Court Act provides. The Court with original and appellate jurisdiction to hear and determine all disputes in accordance with Article 162(2)(b) of the Constitution and with the provisions of this Act or any other law applicable in Kenya relating to environment and land.[273]

2. **Power to hear and determine disputes relating to environmental planning and protection**

Within the scope of its authority as defined by Article 162(2)(b) of the Constitution, the Court possesses the capacity to adjudicate disputes encompassing a diverse range of environmental and land-related matters. This encompasses issues such as environmental planning and protection, climate concerns, land use planning, title, tenure, boundaries, rates, rents, valuations, mining, minerals, and other natural resources. Additionally, the Court is empowered to address disputes related to the compulsory acquisition of land, matters associated with land administration and management, disputes concerning public, private, and community land, as well as conflicts arising from contracts, choses in action, or other instruments that confer enforceable interests in land. The court's jurisdiction is expansive and extends to any other disputes directly linked to environmental and land issues.[274]

---

[271] Article 162(2) (b) of the Constitution and Section 13 of the Environment and Land Court Act.

[272] Article 162(2) (b) of the Constitution

[273] Section 13(1) of the Environment and Land Court Act.

[274] Section 13(2) of the Environment and Land Court Act.

3. Redress of a denial, violation or infringement of, or threat to, rights or fundamental freedom

The Court is further authorized to hear and decide on applications seeking redress for the denial, violation, infringement, or threat to rights or fundamental freedoms associated with a clean and healthy environment. This authority is derived from Articles 42, 69, and 70 of the Constitution. The Court is thus vested with the responsibility to address and remedy situations where individuals allege that their constitutional rights to a clean and healthy environment, as outlined in these specific articles,

have been transgressed or are under threat."[275] Article 165(5) of the Constitution divests the High Court the jurisdiction in respect of matters falling within the jurisdiction of the courts contemplated

under Article 162(2) of the Constitution.[276]

4.14. The Jurisdiction and status of Environmental and Lands Court.

International standards in environmental justice serve as vital frameworks that guide nations in addressing environmental issues in a fair and equitable manner. These standards, often derived from international agreements and conventions, provide guidelines for sustainable development, pollution control, and community participation. Nations use these standards to shape their domestic environmental policies, ensuring alignment with global goals for environmental protection and social justice.

A.) status of Environmental and Lands Court.

In the context of Kenya, the Environmental and Land Court (ELC) holds a critical jurisdictional role. Established under the Environmental and Land

Court Act of 2011, this specialized court deals exclusively with environmental and land-related disputes.[277] It possesses the authority to hear cases pertaining to environmental conservation, natural resource management, land use planning, and disputes arising from environmental laws. The ELC acts as a significant mechanism for enforcing environmental justice within the country, offering a dedicated forum where environmental disputes are adjudicated, thereby contributing to the effective implementation of international standards and ensuring the protection of both the environment and the rights of Kenyan citizens.

B.) Jurisdiction of Environmental and Lands Court.

The Environmental courts and tribunals that deal exclusively with environmental matters and interpret the rule of law as provided by the Kenyan Constitution of 2010, as well as other

[275] Section 13 (3) of the Environment and Land Court Act. [276] Republic vs. Karisa Chengo & 2 Others [2017] eKLR [277] Section 13 of the Environment and Land Court Act (1)

supplementary legislation in form of acts of parliament, that operationalize judicial and quasi-judicial institutions in the environmental justice system. The judiciary therefore plays an important role in the interpretation, explanation and enforcement of laws and regulations.

1.) Power to Hear and Determine Environmental Disputes.

The court possesses the power to hear and determine disputes relating to environmental planning and protection, climate issues, land use planning, title, tenure, boundaries, rates, rents, valuations, mining, minerals and other natural resources as well as disputes relating to compulsory acquisition of land, land administration and management, disputes relating to public, private and community land and contracts, choses in action or other instruments granting any enforceable interest in land and any other dispute relating to environment and land.[278]

2.) CIVIL AND CRIMINAL JURISDICTION.

An in depth overview of the statutory and constitutional framework of the jurisdiction of the Environment and Land Court leads to the conclusion that Environment and Land Court as contemplated under Article 162(2)(b) of the Constitution, has broad constitutional jurisdiction to hear and determine disputes relating to the environment and the use, occupation, and title to land. The Constitution has thus donated powers to Parliament to formulate a legal order particularizing the broad constitutional framework.[279] In actualizing this constitutional mandate, parliament in its legislative wisdom has provided in Section 13(7) of the Environment and Land Court Act broad powers to the Court to make any order or grant any relief the Court deems fit and just. The reliefs provided for under the Act include interim and permanent preservation orders.

3.) Criminal Jurisdiction of the Environment and Land court.

Criminal enforcement of environmental law is necessary to protect the integrity of the regulatory system, prevent harm to the environment and to punish the violators, it is for this reason that Article 42 of the Constitution obligates the State, including the 1st Respondent, to protect the right to a clean and healthy environment through legislative measures.[280] The Environment and Land court is often at times called upon to settle disputes relating to the environment and the use and title to land. Some disputes involve adverse and rival contentions of fraud especially relating to fraudulent

---

[278] Section 13(1) of The Environmental and Land Court Act.

[279] National Land Commission v Afrison Export Import Limited& 10 others [2019] eKLR (para. 8)

[280]Patricia Kameri-Mbote; 'the use of Criminal Law in Enforcing Environmental Law'; in Environmental Governance in Kenya, Implementing the Framework Law, ed. C.O. Okidi, et al.

titles. When the court adjudicates over rival titles to determine between *bona fide* and fraudulent title it traverses over aspects of fraud that constitutes a criminal offence. The court is therefore at liberty to exercise its jurisdiction under Section 13(7) of the Environment and Land Court Act and to issue conservatory orders relating to both civil and criminal processes, relating to any impugned title facing allegations of fraud, as well as in cases where the court is required, to exercise judicial review jurisdiction, in criminal proceedings on criminal offences under the Environmental Management and Coordination Act (the EMCA) as well as other relevant statutes.

4.) The Implication of the Jurisdiction Under Section 13(7) of The Environment and Land Act.

The provision of section 13(7) implies that the statutory authority to grant interim or permanent

preservation orders is not limited to civil processes only. The court thus holds the power to issue preservation orders that extend beyond civil processes. The environment and Land Court is thus empowered under Section 13(7)(a) of the Environment and Land Court Act to issue preservatory orders in both civil and criminal processes. It should most importantly be noted that this jurisdiction is only limited to matters relating to environment and the use and occupation, and title to land.

5.) Appellate Jurisdiction of the Environment and Land Court.

The environment and Land Court exercises appellate authority over the decisions of local Environmental, tribunals in respect of matters falling within the jurisdiction of the Court. The Environment and Land Court plays a crucial role in the legal system, specifically in its capacity as an appellate authority. This means that it has the important responsibility of reviewing and reconsidering decisions made by local Environmental tribunals. These decisions are typically related to matters that fall within the jurisdiction of the Environment and Land Court. This appellate function implies that the court has the power to assess the judgments and rulings made by local tribunals. This process is essential for ensuring that legal matters are thoroughly examined and justly decided upon, upholding the principles of fairness and justice within the legal system. One of the key functions of the Environment and Land Court is to oversee cases that involve environmental and land-related issues. When disputes arise in these areas, local tribunals handle them in the first instance. However, if any party involved in the case disagrees with the decision made at this level, they have the right to appeal to the Environment and Land Court. In this appellate role, the court reviews the evidence, legal arguments, and procedures followed in the previous hearings. This careful review process ensures that the decisions made are consistent with the law and are based on sound legal principles. Furthermore, the appellate authority of the Environment and Land Court emphasizes the significance of its jurisdiction. Matters concerning the environment and land are often complex and have far-reaching implications for both individuals and communities. By having an appellate body that specializes in these specific areas of law, the legal system can maintain a high standard of expertise and accuracy when dealing with cases related to the environment and land. This specialized focus ensures that the decisions made by the tribunals are well-informed, legally sound, and contribute to the overall fairness and integrity of the judicial process.

4.15. ENVIRONMENTAL TRIBUNALS IN KENYA.

Calls for improved access to environmental justice, the environmental rule of law, sustainable development, a green economy, and climate justice are leading policy makers, decision makers and other stakeholders to the reexamination of the available mechanisms in addressing environmental issues. Stakeholders have in response taken a hard look at their governance institutions and are creating new judicial and administrative bodies to improve access to justice and environmental governance. Environmental Courts and Tribunals are progressively being viewed as the logical solution to the existing barriers in traditional justice systems.[281]

A.) Establishment and authority of environmental Tribunals in Kenya.

The National Environmental Tribunal is established under Section 125 of the Environment Management and Coordination Act of 1999. The National Environmental Tribunal has the authority to hear disputes arising from decisions of the National Environment Management Authority on matters pertaining to the issuance, denial, or revocation of licenses. It also has the mandate of dealing with the offences from the Kenya Wildlife Management Act and the Kenya Forests Act.[282] The major reason Tribunals are progressively being considered as important avenues of environmental justice is because of the flexibility in procedure as compared to ordinary courts which have rigid procedural underpinnings. Considerably, environmental conflicts require quick action or response, which is incompatible with the slow pace of the court system that, due

---

[281] Professors George (Rock) Pring & Catherine (Kitty) Pring, University of Denver Environmental Courts and Tribunal Study and Global Environmental Outcomes LLC. UN Environment guide to Specialized Environmental Courts and Tribunals

[282] Section 125 of the Environment Management and Coordination Act of 1999.

to its bureaucracy and technical rituals, that eventually become an obstacle to effective protection of the environment and to economic progress."[283]

B.) The composition of Kenya's National Environmental Tribunal.

The tribunal consists of one chairperson who is a nominee of the judicial service commission. For appointment the nominee must to be qualified as a judge of the High court of Kenya. The Tribunal also consists an advocate of the High Court of Kenya who is nominated by the Law Society of Kenya, a lawyer with professional qualifications in environmental law who is appointed by the Minister as well as two ministerial appointees who must be persons with an exemplary demonstration of academic competence in the field of environmental management appointed by the Minister.[284]

4.16. Judicial Remedies in the Enforcement of Environmental Justice.

The right to a clean environment is a fundamental right in Kenya, the constitution provides for the right to a lean and healthy environment and the right to have that right protected.[285] The Environmental and Land Court has the jurisdiction to hear and determine applications for redress of a denial, violation or infringement of, or threat to, rights or fundamental freedom relating to a clean and health environment under Articles 42, 69 and 70 of the Constitution.[286]

A.) Strict Liability in Environmental Matters.

Strict liability in environmental matters refers to the legal principle where individuals or entities can be held liable for environmental harm regardless of their intent or negligence. This means that if someone is engaged in an activity that leads to environmental damage, they can be held responsible for the consequences, even if they took all possible precautions to prevent it.[287] Responsibility arising from the nature of a dangerous activity rather than negligence or an intentional act.is also known as strict liability or liability without fault. In some cases, a person or organization can liable for damages to others even if it has not acted negligently or intentionally. This is because some activities are so dangerous that their very existence imposes a greater degree of responsibility on the part of the person conducting the activity. This concept is crucial in

---

[283] Justice Antonio Herman Benjamin, High Court of Brazil, available online at http://digitalcommons.pace.edu/pelr/vol29/iss2/8 at 584.

[284]Section 125(1) of The Environmental Management and Coordination Act of 1999

[285]Article 42 of The Constitution of Kenya 2010

[286]Section 13(3) of the Environmental and Land Court Act.

[287] Environmental Law and Policy" by James Salzman and Barton H. Thompson Jr.

environmental law as it ensures that polluters are held accountable for their actions, encouraging them to adopt practices that minimize environmental harm. Strict liability also simplifies the legal process by eliminating the need to prove fault, making it easier to enforce environmental regulations and protect natural resources. [288] If a person keeps certain element in an unnatural way like a large amount of water or noxious chemical in a restricted area or reservoir, the person is responsible for the danger the element poses, even if the person could not be proved to be negligent.

B.) International Jurisprudence and Precedent on Strict Liability

Ryland's Vs Fletcher

Strict liability has roots in English common law and has been adopted and adapted in various legal systems worldwide. One of the foundational cases in the development of strict liability is *Ryland's v Fletcher (1868) LR 3 HL 330*, a landmark English tort law case that established the principles of strict liability for the escape of dangerous substances. [289] The decision in favor of the petitioner's case held that the true rule of law is that the person who, for his own purposes, brings on his land, and collects and keeps there anything likely to do mischief if it escapes, must keep it at his own peril, and, if he does not do so, he is prima facie answerable for all the damage which is the natural consequence of its escape. He can excuse himself by showing that the escape was owing to the plaintiff's own default, or, perhaps that the escape was a consequence of vis major, or the act of God; but as nothing of this sort exists here, it is unnecessary to inquire what excuse would be sufficient.

The person whose cellar is invaded by the filth of his neighbor's privy, or whose habitation is made unhealthy by the fumes and offensive vapors of his reasonable and just that the neighbor who has brought something on his own property but which he knows will be mischievous if it gets on his neighbor's, should be obliged to make good the damage which ensues if he does not succeed in confining it to his own property. But for his act in bringing it there no mischief would have accrued, and it seems just that he should at his peril keep it there, so that no mischief may accrue, or answer for the natural and anticipated consequences." If it does escape and cause damage, he is

---

[288] Environmental Regulation: Law, Science, and Policy" by Robert V. Percival, Christopher H. Schroeder, Alan S. Miller, and James P. Leape.

[289] Ryland's Vs Fletcher (1861-73) ALL ER REPI is the *Locus o*n the Principle of Strict Liability. Any person who keeps anything in unnatural circumstances has to bear the full consequences of the liability that arises if the things that he keeps escapes to his neighbor's land and causes injury.

responsible, however careful he may have taken to prevent the damage. In considering whether a defendant is liable to a plaintiff for the damage which the plaintiff may have sustained, the question in general is not whether the defendant has acted with due care and caution, but whether his acts have occasioned the damage."[290]

C.) Absolute Liability in Environmental Matters

The Supreme Court of India in *M C Mehta Vs Union of India (1987) 1 SCC 395* introduced the concept of absolute liability here the defendant is engaged in industrial activities resulting in pollution. The court stated thus, "The enterprise must be held to be under an obligation to provide that the hazardous or inherently dangerous activity in which it is engaged must be conducted with the highest standards of safety and if any harm results on account of such activity, the enterprise must be absolutely liable to compensate for such harm and it should be no answer to the enterprise to say that it had taken all reasonable care and that the harm occurred without any negligence on its part. Since the persons harmed on account of the hazardous or inherently dangerous activity carried on by the enterprise would not be in a position to isolate the process of operation from the hazardous preparation of the substance of any other related element that caused the harm, the enterprise must be held strictly liable for causing such harm as part of the social cost of carrying on the hazardous or inherently dangerous activity. If the enterprise is permitted to carry on a hazardous or inherently dangerous activity for its profit, the law must presume that such permission is conditional on the enterprise absorbing the cost of any accident arising on account of such hazardous or inherently dangerous activity as an appropriate item for its overheads. Such hazardous or inherently dangerous activity for private profit can be tolerated on condition that the enterprise engaged in such hazardous or inherently dangerous activity indemnifies all those who suffer on account of carrying on such hazardous or inherently dangerous activity regardless of whether it is carried out carefully or not.[291] we would therefore hold that where an enterprise is engaged in a hazardous or inherently dangerous activity, resulting for example in escape of toxic gas, the enterprise is strictly and absolutely liable to compensate all those who are affected by the accident and such liability is not subject to any of the exceptions which operate vis-à-vis the

---

[290] The court has affirmed the principle of strict liability as relates to the law in Redlands vs. Fletcher in KM & 9 others v Attorney General & 7 Others [2020] eKLR.

[291] MC Mehta Vs Union of India (1987) 1 SCC 395.

tortious principle of strict liability under the rule in Ryland's Vs. Fletcher (1986) LR 3 HL 330, (1861 – 73)."[292]

D.) Significance of The Legal Concept Absolute Liability in Environmental Law

The principle of absolute liability, established in the case of *M.C. Mehta v. Union of India*, is a significant legal concept in environmental law. In this case, the Supreme Court of India held that industries engaged in hazardous activities are strictly and absolutely liable for any damage caused to the environment and public health. Unlike the principle of strict liability, which still allows for certain defenses, absolute liability imposes an unconditional obligation on the part of the industries. The rationale behind this principle is to ensure that those who engage in inherently dangerous activities are held accountable for any harm caused, regardless of the precautions taken. The case exemplifies the commitment to environmental protection and highlights the importance of holding industries accountable for their actions. This principle has been pivotal in shaping environmental regulations and serves as a deterrent for industries to exercise the utmost care and diligence in their operations. Furthermore, this landmark case underscored the judiciary's role in safeguarding the environment and promoting sustainable development, setting a precedent for future cases involving environmental issues in the country.

4.17. Other Statutory Remedies available in the enforcement of Environmental justice in Kenya

The law that guides the enforcement of environmental rights is based on common law principles. The constitution of Kenya sets out judicial remedies that suffice in case of infringement. The constitution empowers the environmental courts in accordance with article 165 of the constitution of Kenya 2010 to hear and determine applications for redress or of a denial or violation or infringement or threat to the right to a clean and healthy environment. [293] Judicial remedies emanate from Kenya's Constitution. In any action or proceedings before a court, the court is authorized to grant appropriate reliefs in the form of declaratory orders, Conservatory orders, Injunctions, orders for Compensation. As well as an order for Judicial review.[294] Section 13(7) of the Land and Environment Act empowers the court in exercise of its jurisdiction to issue any order and grant any relief as the Court deems fit and just, including interim or permanent preservation

[292] The Supreme Court of India has emphasized the concept of Absolute liability in the case of MC Mehta Vs Union of India (1987) 1 SCC 395.

[293] Constitution of Kenya 2010, Article 22(1)

[294] Constitution of Kenya 2010, Article 22 (3)

orders such as injunctions, prerogative orders, award of damages, compensation, specific performance, restitution or declaration of costs.[295]

4.14. The Intersection of Common Law Principles Under International Environmental Law.

The Development and Evolution of Common law principles in international environmental law have evolved over time, drawing upon precedents and legal doctrines from various jurisdictions. This development is shaped by international treaties, customary international law, and decisions of international courts and tribunals.[296]

a.) Sovereignty and Shared Resources - Common law principles recognize the tension between state sovereignty and the need for international cooperation in managing shared environmental resources. Concepts like the "no harm" rule establish obligations for states to prevent transboundary harm arising from their activities.[297]

b.) Precautionary Principle - Common law principles incorporate the precautionary principle, emphasizing preventive action in the face of uncertain environmental risks. This principle guides decision-making in areas where scientific understanding is incomplete but potential risks are significant.[298]

4. Equity and Environmental Justice - Common law principles underscore the importance of equity and environmental justice. This includes considerations of historical responsibility, acknowledging that developed countries often bear greater responsibility for environmental degradation and should take proportionate actions.[299]

5. Compliance and Dispute Resolution - Common law principles provide a framework for compliance mechanisms and dispute resolution in international environmental matters. This involves procedures for resolving conflicts between states, ensuring adherence to environmental agreements, and holding parties accountable for violations.[300]

---

[295] The Land and Environment Act, Section 13(7)

[296] Sands, Philippe, and Pierre Klein. "Bowett's Law of International Institutions." (2009).

[297] Brown Weiss, Edith. "In Fairness to Future Generations: International Law, Common Patrimony, and Intergenerational Equity." (1989).

[298] Sand, Peter H., and Marc B. Maresca. "The Precautionary Principle and International Law: The Challenge of Implementation." (2002).

[299] Boyle, Alan E., and Michael R. Anderson. "Human Rights Approaches to Environmental Protection." (2008).

[300] Epps, Tracey. "Environmental Compliance in International Law: Lessons from the WTO." (2006).

4.19. The Intersection of Common Law Principles Under Kenyan Law. a.) Nuisance Under the Public Health Act.

Some provisions of the Public Health Act provides guidelines regarding waste management and disposal, Section 118 lists activities that are regarded as a nuisance.[301] Such acts include the discharge of poisonous substances such as waste water from any premise into the environment or into a water course and irrigation channel that is not designed for such disposal.[302] The provisions also classify the accumulation and depositing of refuse that is injurious or dangerous to health as an environmental nuisance .[303] Public health officers are empowered to notify and order persons or entities whose activities cause such nuisance to remove the nuisance.[304]

b.) Negligence

When an individual fail to exercise reasonable care in situations where such care is expected, their actions or inaction can be classified as negligence. According to common law principles, negligence occurs when there is a legal duty of care, and the person in question, under the given circumstances, fails to provide the standard of care required to fulfill a specific obligation. If this failure to meet the legal duty results in harm and injury, negligence is established. In essence, negligence arises from the breach of a legal duty of care, leading to harmful consequences.

If the individual responsible for a nuisance neglects to promptly address and rectify the issue, and in doing so exhibits negligence, the health officer is obligated to file a complaint with a magistrate. This action initiates the process of summoning the individual before the magistrate's court to address the matter.[305] The court, through the issuance of such an order, holds the authority to levy a fine on the individual, with the fine not surpassing two hundred shillings. Additionally, the court can provide instructions regarding the payment of costs incurred up to the point of the hearing and the issuance of the order for the removal of the nuisance.[306]

---

[301] Section 118 of the public Health Act

[302] Section 118 (e) Ibid

[303] Section 118 (h) Ibid

[304] Section 119 Ibid

[305] Section 120 (1) Ibid

[306] Section 120(3) Ibid

c.) Gross Negligence

In circumstances where an individual act in a manner that depicts a total indifference for the well- being of others, such actions constitute gross negligence. The punishment and penalty is greater in circumstances where gross negligence is adduced.

4.20. JUDICIAL CHALLENGES IN THE ENFORCEMENT OF ENVIRONMENTAL JUSTICE

Environmental justice faces a myriad of challenges in Kenya, most of the challenges are either administrative, technical procedural or financial in nature, this is because the concept of environmental justice is relatively new in Kenya and is slowly gaining impetus, the introduction of Environmental and Land courts is nevertheless gaining recognition because of its authoritative role though it lacks sufficient technical experts with the technical know-how and abilities in the science of environmental matters. Other challenges include;

1.Rigidity In The Enforcement Of Judicial Rules And   Procedures

Lack of flexibility in court rules and procedures that make it impossible to respond to international environmental laws and standards, to provide alternative dispute resolution options, to encourage public participation in the process of decision making, to ensure public access to information, or to be transparent and accountable to the public.

2.   **Limited Knowledge in the areas of International Environmental law and National Environmental law.**

International environmental law and national environmental law are important legal instruments in the enforcement of environmental justice. One of the challenges in the areas of environmental justice is the limited knowledge amongst key stakeholders and the public on the available legislative frameworks and principles that guide judicial institutions and authorities in decision making, limited knowledge on the part of judicial officers also impedes environmental justice as the officers are unaware and unable to apply sound legal principles in order to make sound decisions. The environment and land courts under the constitution of Kenya 2010 seek to achieve efficient and sound environmental justice through the delineation of the special courts that are required to have competent judges knowledgeable in the areas of environmental law. The challenge however remains in most jurisdictions that do not have such special courts and in whose jurisdiction, they see and find little attention or significance to environmental issues.

3.   **High costs of litigation in the areas of environmental law.**

The high costs of litigation in the areas of environmental law are an obstacle to the realization of environmental justice. The prohibitive nature of the costs of litigation in the areas of environmental law is largely because of the technical aspects involved in the determination of the issues that suffice in environmental disputes. Technical aspects such as pollution and Environmental Impact Assessment require technical expertise in the preparation and interpretation. The voluminous nature of technical material requires many advocates and experts to prepare and present. These aspects all accumulate increased costs that are borne by the litigants, litigation in environmental issues is hence expensive and prohibitive. For the effective actualization of the right to a clean and healthy environment and the realization of environmental justice there must be efforts to promote public interest litigation as well as affordable access to justice by stakeholders and state machinery.

4. **Lack of Prioritization of Environmental cases.**

The judicialization of environmental issues is a fairly new concept in Kenya. Most disputes of an environmental nature were addressed in civil courts before the promulgation of the new constitution. Most litigants and stakeholders may not fathom that environmental issues are constitutional issues that touch on constitutional as well as fundamental rights that need to be resolved expeditiously. The pendency of environmental disputes in courts for long periods of time is therefore because of lack of prioritization over other matters that are considered urgent and significant.

5. **Limited remedies in the enforcement of environmental awards and disputes.**

one of the key obstacles in the enforcement of environmental awards and disputes is the available remedies in the enforcement of environmental awards. While courts and Tribunals may arrive at awards from the multiple disputes that are litigated within the corridors of justice, moreover the interlocutory injunctions and conservatory orders that subsist are temporary in nature. It is therefore necessary to review the legislative and judicial remedies available to litigants to provide a more robust dispute resolution mechanism that is responsive to the needs of the public.

6. **Undue Delays in the determination of environmental disputes.**

In countries such as Kenya where there are limited resources and the judicial arm of government operates on the whims of the executive, there is an extreme congestion in the corridors of justice. Cases take many years to settle and, in the meantime, litigants continue to suffer loss as they wait upon the decisions of the courts. Some judicial remedies such as injunctions and conservatory orders suffice but they are not as satisfactory as the conclusive determination of disputes and the ultimate closure of disputes. The wheels of justice hence move slowly and generally justice delayed is justice denied.

7. Limited public awareness on the availability of environmental rights and justice.

The lack of awareness on the part of the public and other stakeholders on the available statutory remedies as well as special courts and other quasi-judicial institutions such as environmental tribunals that deal with environmental matters pose a challenge to the achievement of environmental justice. There is therefore a need for the state and other stakeholders to institute measures that will promote awareness among the public and other stakeholders on the right to a clean and healthy environment as well as the available judicial processes and statutory remedies in case of violation or the danger of violation of environmental rights as well as other aspects that fall under the jurisdiction of the Environment and Lands Court.

4.21. Recommendations for Improvement of Judicial Trends Towards promoting Environmental Justice

1. **Promote the environmental rule of law at the national level and international levels and ensure equal access to justice. (SDG target 16.3).**

In order to achieve the Sustainable development goals the aspects of sound environmental justice must be promoted at all levels and jurisdictions, it involves sustained efforts to emphasize, support and promote the environmental rule of law at national, regional and international levels This is attainable through political and legislative good will as well as the institution of fiscal and strategic policies that aim to revive or enhance institutional independence as well as functionality to ensure access to justice by all.[307]

2. **Development of effective, robust,**

**accountable, and transparent institutions
at all levels. (SDG target 16.6).**

There is an urgent need to develop effective and more transparent institutions at all levels to facilitate the adjudication of environmental disputes as well as the enforcement of awards from judicial institutions. State authorities and agencies must emphasize and circumvent corruption and opaqueness in the dealings of judicial and quasi-judicial institutional and other institutions that handle environmental matters, specific emphasis and attention should be directed towards innovative, sustainable and cost effective methods of dispute resolution that inspire confidence

---

[307] United Nations. (2015). Transforming our World: The 2030 Agenda for Sustainable Development. Resolution adopted by the General Assembly on 25 September 2015. A/RES/70/1.

through accountable and transparent dealings. Institutions must mandatorily base their decisions on the rule of law and enable the access of justice to all persons be as effective as possible.[308]

3. **Facilitating public access to information and protection of fundamental freedoms, in accordance with national legislation and international agreements. (SDG target 16.7).**

Access to information is a key aspect for sound and effective decision making. Information is an essential input for the formulation of policy as well as the determination and resolution of disputes. The state and other non-state agencies and actors must promote a culture of transparency and readiness to provide access to information to guide citizens in decision making and other actors in policy formulation. An endeavor must be committed towards protecting fundamental freedoms in accordance with international and national law, compliance with the rule of law and promoting effective preservation of human rights such as the right to equality, access to justice, right to a clean and healthy environment promote effective adjudication of environmental justice. [309]

4. **Promoting and enforcing non-discriminatory laws and policies for sustainable - development.**

Equality is an important element of the rule of law in democratic societies as it promotes equal treatment of all persons before the law. Our constitutional order affirms the principle of equality under article 27 of the constitution and prohibits any manner of discrimination based on any grounds. The enforcement of non-discriminatory laws and policies is critical in the accomplishment of sustainable development goals as it enhances equal access to justice. Members of the public must have faith in the independence and impartiality of the court systems as well as other judicial institutions. These elements buttress the quest for effective environmental justice.[310]

6. Promoting responsive, inclusive, participatory, and representative decision-making at all levels.

For effective access to environmental justice there is a need to promote public participation among all stakeholders in decision making for inclusive environmental governance. Public participation is a fundamental principle of our national ethos and is entrenched in our constitutional order. The constitution requires public authorities to involve members of the public in decision making processes. Public participation in environmental affairs is specifically important as decisions affect

---

[308] United Nations. (2015). Transforming our World: The 2030 Agenda for Sustainable Development. Resolution adopted by the General Assembly on 25 September 2015. A/RES/70/1. [309] *Ibidem*
[310] *Ibidem*

citizens directly, there input in matters that affect their social economic lives is therefore imperative as it facilitates and legitimizes quality decision making.[311]

7. Supporting and promoting the dissemination of information on environmental matters to the public and other stakeholders.

Environmental information is critical in decision making for the public and for purposes of policy formulation and resource mobilization for state agencies and other stakeholders, for equitable and effective access to justice there is an immediate need to facilitate the dissemination of information to all stakeholders. Relevant information on the state of the environment, natural resources, and the impact of industrial and other economic activity upon the environment should be mandatorily provided within a reasonable timeframe and in easily accessible formats most preferably electronic formats on platforms such as social media upon request or in the interest of transparency and social responsibility. Such dissemination of information promotes effective environmental governance and sound decision making in environmental choices. The incentivization of environmental information disclosure for non-state actors and the legislation of compulsory disclosure of relevant information are possible policy reform recommendations for effective dissemination of information among policy makers.[312]

4. Supporting and promoting resource development especially human resource through capacity building in the areas of environmental governance.

It is paramount for the public, the state,

and all other stakeholders to promote resource mobilization and human resource development in environmental governance and adjudication. Generally environmental adjudication requires competent human resource in judges and other technical experts who understand the scientific as well as legal implications of environmental aspects. Vocational and higher education should formulate curricular to reflect societal needs that stimulate the innovation of sustainable solutions to both legal and scientific environmental problems. Continuous professional development for judges and magistrates is important in enlightening members of the bench on the progressive trends around the globe and on innovative environmental solutions in the adjudication of environmental disputes.[313]

---

[311] *Ibidem*
[312] *Ibidem*
[313] *Ibidem*

9. Promoting revolutionary and progressive jurisprudence in the scope of environmental litigation and justice.

Environmental jurisprudence is rapidly growing as the area of environmental law and governance receives its rightful attention. Many countries are adopting revolutionary principles in the application of law in environmental matters as well as the resolution of disputes. Whilst common law principles involve technical and conservative approaches that require the strict interpretation and application of the law. Revolutionary principles promote environmental conservation and public interest. One of such revolutionary principles from common law involve the principle of absolute liability that does not allow any exceptions for environmental harm occasioned by the escape of unnaturally held elements. Such revolutionary principle is important in deterring environmental degradation as well as negligence in environmental guardianship.

Environmental justice demands many dynamics including the legal frameworks, societal engagement, and framework of international cooperation in the pursuit of a sustainable future and transformational environmental justice. In the face of daunting obstacles, the pursuit of environmental justice emerges as a balance between legal resilience and societal consciousness. While the remedies for environmental injustices and the pursuit of these undertakings promise a path toward a fairer, ecologically balanced world. There is a pressing need for innovative strategies, inclusive policies, and unwavering global collaboration. for collective responsibility to unite in their commitment to forging a harmonious relationship between humanity and nature.

BIBLIOGRAPHY

1. Convention on Biological Diversity (1992). Retrieved from https://www.cbd.int/convention/

2. Britannica Encyclopedia 2023 Definition of the Term 'Environment'. Retrieved from [https://www.britannica.com/dictionary/environment]

3. Oxford English Dictionary 2023 Definition of the Term 'Environment'. Retrieved from [https://www.oed.com/?tl=true]

4. Ronald B. Mitchell, et al., The International Environmental Agreement Database Project (2010). Available online at [http://iea.uoregon.edu/page.php?query=static&file=definitions.htm]

5. French Dictionary 2023 Definition of the word 'Environner'. Retrieved from [https://www.larousse.fr/dictionnaires/francais/environner/30158]

6. Louka, E 2006. International Environmental Law: Fairness, Effectiveness, and World Order. Cambridge University Press.

7. Trail Smelter Arbitration (United States v. Canada), 3 U.N.R.I.A.A. 1905 (1941). Trail Smelter case, 16 April 1938, 11 March 1941, 3 RIAA 1907 (1941); R. M. Bratspies and R. A. Miller (eds.), Transboundary Harm in International Law: Lessons from the Trail Smelter Arbitration (2006).

8. Ved P. Nanda George, (Rock) Pring. International Environmental Law and Policy for the 21st Century 2nd Revised Edition.

9. United Nations, 2007. "Report of the United Nation's Award between the United States and the United Kingdom relating to the rights of jurisdiction of United States in the Bering's sea and the preservation of fur seals." Retrieved from [https://legal.un.org/riaa/cases/vol_XXVIII/263-276.pdf]

10. Maria Alzira Pimenta Dinis, "Environment and Human Health." Journal of Environment Pollution and Human Health, vol. 4, no. 2 (2016): 52-59. DOI: 10.12691/jephh-4-2-3

11. Poore, J., and T. Nemecek. "Reducing Food's Environmental Impacts Through Producers and Consumers." 27 April 2021. [https://

www.science.org/doi/10.1126/
science.aaq0216#:~:text=]

12.   United Nations. "Foreword to 'Environment, Religion and Culture in the Context of the 2030 Agenda for Sustainable Development'." UNEP, 2016. [https://wedocs.unep.org/bitstream/ handle/20.500.11822/8696/- Environment, _religion_and_culture_in_the_context_of_the203 0_agenda_for_sustainable development-]

13.   Encyclopedia Britannica. "Internet." Encyclopedia Britannica, 8th ed., vol.9, 2009.

14. Salmond, J. W. (1966). Salmond on Jurisprudence. London: Sweet & Maxwell.

15.   Timo Koivurova. Basic issues in international environmental law Page 8.

16. Bouchet-Saulnier, Françoise. The Practical Guide to Humanitarian Law. Rowman & Littlefield Publishers, 1998.

17. International Court of Justice. "Advisory Opinion regarding the Legality of the Threat or Utilization of Nuclear Armament." Para 29. Advisory Opinion of 8 July 1996.

18. Anthony D'Amato, The Concept of Custom in International Law (1971)

19. The North Sea Continental Shelf cases, ICJ Reps, 1969, p. 3 at 44.

20.   International Court of Justice Statute. Article 38: "The Court, whose function is to decide in accordance with international law such disputes as are submitted to it, shall apply: a. international conventions, whether general or particular, establishing rules expressly recognized by the contesting states; b. international custom, as evidence of a general practice accepted as law; c. the general principles of law recognized by civilized nations; d. subject to

the provisions of Article 59, judicial decisions and the teachings of the most highly qualified publicists of the various nations, as subsidiary means for the determination of rules of law."

21. Orellana, Marcos A. "Typology of Instruments of Public Environmental International Law." Digital repository Beta, Page 8, paragraph 4.
22. United Nations Environmental Programme. Environmental Rule of Law: First Global Report. UNEP,www.unep.org/resources/assessment/environmental-rule-law-first-global-.
23. Koivurova, Timo. Introduction to International Environmental Law. Routledge, 2013.
24. Lomborg, Bjørn. The Skeptical Environmentalist: Measuring the Real State of the World. Cambridge: Cambridge University Press, 2001. (Preface).
25. Kiss, Alexandre, and Dinah Shelton. Guide to International Environmental Law. Page 240, paragraph 3.
26. United Nations Environment Programme. Judicial Handbook. Page 4.
27. Vienna Convention on the Law of Treaties. Article 27 and 46.
28. The Constitution of Kenya 2010. Sixth Schedule.
29. Kiss, Alexandre, and Dinah Shelton. Guide to International Environmental Law. Page 12, paragraph 2.
30. La Grande Case (Germany v. United States), 2001 ICJ (June 27), 40 ILM 1069 (2001).
31. Article 70 of the Kenyan constitution of 2010
32. Sachs, Aron. The Humboldt Current: Nineteenth-Century Exploration and the Roots of American Environmentalism. New York: Viking, 2006.
33. Bodansky, Daniel. The Art and Craft of International Environmental Law. Harvard University Press, 2010.
34. Kronman, Anthony T. Max Weber. Stanford, CA: Stanford University Press, 1983.
35. Koivurova, Timo. Introduction to International Environmental Law. Page 2.
36. Croxton, Derek. "The Peace of Westphalia of 1648 and the Origins of Sovereignty." The International

History Review, vol. 21, no. 3, Sep. 1999, pp. 569-591.

37. Marine Mammal Commission. "Assessing the Long-term Effects of the BP Deepwater Horizon Oil Spill on Marine Mammals in the Gulf of Mexico." August 2011, [https://www.mmc.gov/wp- content/uploads/longterm_effects_bp_oilspil.pdf]

38. Leigh Day. "Oil Spills on the Niger Delta." Leigh Day, [https://www.leighday.co.uk/news/cases-and-testimonials/cases/shell-bodo/].

39. Kiss, Alexandre, and Dinah Shelton. Guide to International Environmental Law. Page 11, paragraph 3.

40. Karl, T.R., and Trenberth, K.E. "Modern Global Climate Change." Science, vol. 302, no. 5651, 2003, pp. 1719-1723. doi:10.1126/science.1090228.

41. The International Energy Association IEA 2009

42. The Essential Principles of Climate Literacy. "Climate.gov, [https://www.climate.gov/Teaching/climate#:~:text=Essential%20Principle%206%3A%20H uman%20activities,impacts%20throughout%20the%20Earth%20system.]

43. Diamond, Jared. The Last Tree on Easter Island. Penguin Classics, 2021.

44. Brown Weiss, Edith. "International Environmental Law: Contemporary Issues and the Emergence of a New World Order" (1993). Georgetown Law Faculty Publications and Other Works, paper 1628.

45. Kiss, Alexandre, and Dinah Shelton. Guide to International Environmental Law. Page 176, paragraph 2.

46. Pedraza, Jorge Morales. "World Major Nuclear Accidents and Their Negative Impact on The Environment, Human Health, And Public Opinion." IJEEE, vol. 21, no. 2, ISSN: 1054-853X.

47. UNESCO. "Mijikenda Kaya Forests." UNESCO World Heritage Centre, [whc.unesco.org/en/list/1231].

48. Bodansky, Daniel. The Art and Craft of International Environmental Law. Page 22, paragraph 3.

49. United States General Accounting Office (GAO), International Agreements Are Not Well Monitored (GAO-RCED-92–43, 1992).

50. Langkawi Declaration on the Environment.

51. Nagtzaam, Gerry, Evan van Hook, and Douglas Guilfoyle. International Environmental Law: A Case Study Analysis. Page 2.

52. The United Nations Charter. Article 2.

53. Kiss, Alexandre, and Dinah Shelton. Guide to International Environmental Law. Page 11, paragraph 3.

54. Convention on Biological Diversity. Preamble. 1992.

55. The Stockholm Declaration on the Human Environment. Principle 21. 1972.

56. The Rio Declaration on Environment and Development. Principle 7. 1992.

57. The United Nations Framework Convention on Climate Change. Article 3. 1992.

58. Louka, Elli. International Environmental Law. Page 18, paragraph 3.

59. The Constitution of Kenya. Article 42.

60. Article 12 Ibid

61. Kiss, Alexander, and Dinah Shelton. Guide to International Environmental Law. Page 11, paragraph 3.

62. The Vietnamese Ministry of Natural Resources and Environment, Department of Legal Affairs Handbook, titled International Environmental Law: Multilateral Environmental Agreements, Page 10, Paragraph 1.

63. United Nations Charter. Art. 2, para. 3.

64. Bernie, Patricia, Alan Boyle, and Catherine Redgwell. International Law and the Environment. 3rd ed., Oxford University Press, 2009.

65. Brierly, J.L. The Outlook for International Law. Oxford at the Clarendon Press, 1944.

66. Shelton, Dinah, and Alexandre Charles Kiss. Judicial Handbook on Environmental Law. Introduction by Hon. Judge Christopher G. Weeramantry. UNEP, 2005.
67. Elli Louka, 'Introduction to International Environmental Law,' page 18, Para.
68. Edith Brown Weiss, 'The Evolution of International Environmental Law' Japanese Yearbook of International Law, 54 (2011): 1.
69. Peter H Sand, 'Origin and History in 'The Oxford Handbook of International Environmental Law,' Page 50.
70. The 1902 Convention for the Protection of Birds Useful to Agriculture (Paris, Mar. 19, 1902)
71. The treaties entered between the United States and Canada include the United States-Canada Agreement Regarding the Establishment of Joint Pollution Contingency Plans for pollution from Oil and Other Noxious Substances (June 19, 1974), 25 UST 1280, TIAS 7861; United States-Canada Agreement on Great Lakes Water Quality with Annexes (Nov. 22, 1978), 30 U.S.T. 1383, TIAS No. 9257, amended Oct. 16, 1983, TIAS No. 10798.
72. International Union for Conservation of Nature. "Convention relative to the Preservation of Fauna and Flora in their Natural State." IUCN, TRE-000069, 8 Nov. 1933.
73. Convention on Nature Protection and Wildlife Preservation in the Western Hemisphere." 56 Stat. 1354. U.S. Fish and Wildlife Service.
74. Introduction to World Forestry. Jack C. Westoby. Basil Blackwell. 1989.

75. Preamble of the Convention Relative to the Preservation of Fauna and Flora in their Natural State." Enacted on 8 Nov. 1933, University of Oslo Library, www.jus.uio.no/english/services/library/treaties/06/6-02/preservation-fauna-natural.html.

76. Article 2 Preamble of the Convention Relative to the Preservation of Fauna and Flora in their Natural State." Enacted on 8 Nov. 1933, University of Oslo Library, www.jus.uio.no/english/services/library/treaties/06/6-02/preservation-fauna-natural.html.

77. Article 2 (2) Preamble of the Convention Relative to the Preservation of Fauna and Flora in their Natural State." Enacted on 8 Nov. 1933, University of Oslo Library, www.jus.uio.no/english/services/library/treaties/06/6-02/preservation-fauna-natural.html.

78. Definition of natural reserves according to the convention on the Preservation of Fauna and Flora in their Natural State of 1933

79. UCN. "Protected Area Category." IUCN, [https://www.iucn.org/theme/protected-areas/our-work/protected-area-categories.]

80. Vietnamese Ministry of Natural Resources and Environment, Department of Legal Affairs. "International Environmental Law Multilateral Environmental Agreements." Page 10, para. 4.

81. Ministry of Natural Resources and Environment, Department of Legal Affairs. "International Environmental Law: Multilateral Environmental Agreements." International Publishing House, 2017, p. 27.

82. U.N. F. COSOC, Annexes, Agenda Item 12 (Doc. E/4466/Add.$) at 2 (1968).

83. The Evolution of International Environmental Law *Edith Brown Weiss Georgetown University Law Center, weiss@law.georgetown.edu available online at https://scholarship.law.georgetown.edu/facpub/1669/

84. Elli Louka, International Environmental Law-Fairness, Effectiveness, and World Order, page 12.

85. Yann Kerbrat, Sandrine Maljean-Dubois. The Role of International Law in the Promotion of the

Precautionary Principle. Carina Costa de Oliveira, Gabriela G. B. Lima Moraes, Fabrício Ramos Ferreira (dir.), A interpretação do princípio da precaução no direito brasileiro, no direito comparado e no direito internacional, Pontes, pp. 275-284, 2019. ffhalshs-02342746f

86. United Nations. "Paragraph 77." Conference Document A/CONF.48/PC/57.

87. Strong, Maurice F. Statement before the Second Committee of the General Assembly. 19 Oct. 1972, pp. 2-3. (Mimeo.)

88. Kiss, Alexandre, and Dinah Shelton. Guide to International Environmental Law. Page 90, para. 1..

89. Stockholm Convention on Persistent Organic Pollutants. "Principles 2 and 5." UNEP, www.pops.int/..

90. Stockholm Convention on Persistent Organic Pollutants. "Principles 3" UNEP, www.pops.int/..

91. Stockholm Convention on Persistent Organic Pollutants. "Principles 4." UNEP, www.pops.int/..

92. Stockholm Convention on Persistent Organic Pollutants. "Principles 9." UNEP, www.pops.int/..

93. Stockholm Convention on Persistent Organic Pollutants. "Principles 10." UNEP, www.pops.int/..

94. Stockholm Convention on Persistent Organic Pollutants. "Principles 11." UNEP, www.pops.int/..

95. Stockholm Convention on Persistent Organic Pollutants. "Principles 12." UNEP, www.pops.int/..

96. Stockholm Convention on Persistent Organic Pollutants. "Principles 13." UNEP, www.pops.int/..

97. Stockholm Convention on Persistent Organic Pollutants. "Principles 14." UNEP, www.pops.int/..

98.   Stockholm Convention on Persistent Organic Pollutants. "Principles 15." UNEP, www.pops.int/..

99.   Stockholm Convention on Persistent Organic Pollutants. "Principles 16." UNEP, www.pops.int/..

100.   Stockholm Convention on Persistent Organic Pollutants. "Principles 17." UNEP, www.pops.int/..

101.   Stockholm Convention on Persistent Organic Pollutants. "Principles 18." UNEP, www.pops.int/..

102.   Stockholm Convention on Persistent Organic Pollutants. "Principles 19." UNEP, www.pops.int/..

103.   Stockholm Convention on Persistent Organic Pollutants. "Principles 20." UNEP, www.pops.int/..

104.   Stockholm Convention on Persistent Organic Pollutants. "Principles 21." UNEP, www.pops.int/..

105.   Stockholm Convention on Persistent Organic Pollutants. "Principles 22." UNEP, www.pops.int/..

106.   Stockholm Convention on Persistent Organic Pollutants. "Principles 24" UNEP, www.pops.int/..

107.   Stockholm Convention on Persistent Organic Pollutants. "Principles 25." UNEP, www.pops.int/..

108.   Stockholm Convention on Persistent Organic Pollutants. "Principles 26." UNEP, www.pops.int/..

109.   Stockholm Convention on Persistent Organic Pollutants. "Principles 25." UNEP, www.pops.int/."

110.   Stockholm Convention on Persistent Organic Pollutants. "Principles 26." UNEP, www.pops.int/."

111.   United Nations. "The Rio Declaration on Environment and Development: Principle 1." UnitedNationsSustainableDevelopment KnowledgePlatform,www.un.org/en/development/

desa/population/migration/generalassembl y/docs/
global   compact/
A_CONF.151_26_Vol.I_Declaration.pdf.

112.   United Nations. "The Rio Declaration on Environment
and Development: Principle 2." Ibid

113.   United Nations. "The Rio Declaration on Environment
and Development: Principle 4." Ibid

114.   United Nations. "The Rio Declaration on Environment
and Development: Principle 5." Ibid

115.   United Nations. "The Rio Declaration on Environment
and Development: Principle 6." Ibid

116.   United Nations. "The Rio Declaration on Environment
and Development: Principle 27 Ibid

117.   United Nations. "The Rio Declaration on Environment
and Development: Principle 7 Ibid

118.   United Nations. "The Rio Declaration on Environment
and Development: Principle 8 Ibid

119.   United Nations. "The Rio Declaration on Environment
and Development: Principle 15 Ibid

120.   United Nations. "The Rio Declaration on Environment
and Development: Principle 9 Ibid

121.   United Nations. "The Rio Declaration on Environment
and Development: Principle 10 Ibid

122.   United Nations. "The Rio Declaration on Environment
and Development: Principle 11 Ibid

123.   United Nations. "The Rio Declaration on
Environment and Development: Principle 12 Ibid

124.   United Nations. "The Rio Declaration on
Environment and Development: Principle 13 Ibid

125.   United Nations. "The Rio Declaration on Environment
and Development: Principle 14 Ibid

126.   United Nations. "The Rio Declaration on Environment
and Development: Principle 16 Ibid

127. United Nations. "The Rio Declaration on Environment and Development: Principle 17 Ibid

128. United Nations. "The Rio Declaration on Environment and Development: Principle 18 Ibid

129. United Nations. "The Rio Declaration on Environment and Development: Principle 19 Ibid

130. United Nations. "The Rio Declaration on Environment and Development: Principle 20 Ibid

131. United Nations. "The Rio Declaration on Environment and Development: Principle 21 Ibid

132. United Nations. "The Rio Declaration on Environment and Development: Principle 22 Ibid

133. United Nations. "The Rio Declaration on Environment and Development: Principle 23 Ibid

134. United Nations. "The Rio Declaration on Environment and Development: Principle 24 Ibid

135. United Nations. "The Rio Declaration on Environment and Development: Principle 25 Ibid

136. United Nations. "The Rio Declaration on Environment and Development: Principle 24 Ibid

137. Koivurova, Timo. Introduction to International Environmental Law. Routledge, Taylor & Francis, Page 2, para. 2.

138. Koivurova, Timo. Introduction to International Environmental Law. Routledge, Taylor & Francis, Page 1 Para 3.

139. International Environmental Law Multilateral Environmental Agreements. Page 12, para. 4. Available at. http://www.oas.org/dsd/tool-kit/Documentos/MOduleII/Multilateral%20Environmental%20Agreements.pdf

140. Ibidem

141. sustainable Development in Kenya: Stocktaking in the Run up to Rio+20." United Nations Departmentof Economic and Social Affairs, 2012, https://sustainabledevelopment.un.org/content/documents/985kenya.pdf.

142.

143. Constitution of Kenya 2010, Article 2(5).

144. Constitution of Kenya 2010, Article 2(6).

145. Constitution of Kenya 2010 Article 10.
146. Constitution of Kenya 2010, Article 10.
147. Constitution of Kenya 2010, Article 11(3).
148. Constitution of Kenya 2010, Article 69.
149. Constitution of Kenya 2010, Article 2 (5).
150. Constitution of Kenya 2010, Article 42.
151. Constitution of Kenya 2010, Article 42.
152. Constitution of Kenya 2010, Article 70.
153. Constitution of Kenya 2010, Chapter 5.
154. sustainable Development in Kenya: Stocktaking in the Run up to Rio+20." United Nations Departmentof Economic and Social Affairs, 2012, https://sustainabledevelopment.un.org/content/docuMents/985kenya.pdf.
155. Environmental Management and Coordination Act. Section 3.
156. Environmental Management and Coordination Act, Section 107. 1
157. Introduction to Sustainable Development: A Brief Handbook for Students by Students. International Hellenic University, 2015.
158. Ibidem
159. Pearce, D., & Barbier, E. B. (2000). Blueprint for a sustainable economy. Earthscan Publications.
160. United Nations General Assembly, 1987, p. 43
161. Sen, A. (1999). Development as Freedom. Oxford University Press.
162. Ibidem

163. Carson, Rachel. Silent Spring. First Mariner Books edition, Houghton Mifflin Harcourt, 2002.

164. World Commission on Environment and Development. Our Common Future. Oxford University Press, 1987.

165. Fortun, Kim. Advocacy after Bhopal: Environmentalism, Disaster, New Global Orders. University of Chicago Press, 2001.

166. Ibidem

167. Johnson, Kirsten, "State and community during the aftermath of Mexico City's November 19, 1984 Gas Explosion" (1985). FMHI Publications. 58. https://digitalcommons.Usf.edu/fmhI pub/58

168. International Conference on Chernobyl: Looking Back to go Forward (2005: Vienna, Austria). Proceedings of an International Conference on Chernobyl: Looking Back to Go Forward, organized by the International Atomic Energy Agency on behalf of the Chernobyl Forum and held in Vienna, 6–7 September 2005.

169. World Commission on Environment and Development. Our Common Future. Oxford University Press, 1987, p. 13.

170. Schultz, P.W. (2002). Inclusion with Nature: The Psychology of Human-Nature Relations. In: Schmuck, P., Schultz, W.P. (eds) Psychology of Sustainable Development. Springer, Boston, MA.

171. Hungary v Slovakia), 1997 WL 1168556 (ICJ

172. Dinah L. Shelton & Alex Kiss, Guide to International Environmental Law in Alexandre Kiss, Dinah Shelton, Guide to International Environmental Law (Martinus Nijhoff Publishers, 2007).

173. John Muthui & 19 others v County Government of Kitui & 7 others [2020] eKLR Para 84

174. International Environmental Law-Fairness, Effectiveness, and World Order" by Elli Louka, Page 15. Para 1.

175. Cullet P., Differential Treatment in International Environmental Law and its Contribution to the Evolution of International Law (Aldershot: Ashgate,

2003) pp 8-9).

176. Convention on Biological Diversity. "Sustainable Development Goals." cbd.int, 2020.

177. Daily, G. C. (1997). Nature's services: Societal dependence on natural ecosystems. Island Press.

178. Intergovernmental Panel on Climate Change. Global Warming of 1.5°C. Special Report. IPCC, 2018.

179. Pearce, D., & Barbier, E. B. (2000). Blueprint for a sustainable economy. Earthscan Publications.

180. United Nations Development Programme. Human Development Report 2019: Beyond income, beyond averages, beyond today: Inequalities in human development in the 21st century. UNDP, 2019.

181. Sachs, J. (2005). The End of Poverty: Economic Possibilities for Our Time. Penguin Books.

182. United Nations Environment Programme. Global Resources Outlook 2019: Natural Resources for the Future We Want. UNEP, 2018.

183. Intergovernmental Panel on Climate Change (IPCC). (2014). Climate Change 2014: Mitigation of Climate Change. Cambridge University Press

184. International Energy Agency. Global Energy Review 2021. IEA, 2021.

185. Sustainable practices address climate change by reducing greenhouse gas emissions, promoting renewable energy sources, and implementing energy-efficient technologies

186. Food and Agriculture Organization of the United Nations. The State of Food Security and Nutrition in the World 2020. FAO, 2020.

187. United Nations (UN). (2015). Transforming our world: The 2030 Agenda for Sustainable Development.

188. UN-Water. Integrated Monitoring Guide for SDG 6: Targets and global indicators. UN- Water, 2018.

189. Daily, G. C. (1997). Nature's services: Societal dependence on natural ecosystems. Island Press.

190.United Nations Human Settlements Programme. The State of the World's Cities 2018. UN- Habitat, 2019.

191.United Nations Development Programme (UNDP). (2008). Human Development Report 2007/2008: Fighting climate change: Human solidarity in a divided world.

192. United Nations Educational, Scientific and Cultural Organization. World Heritage and Sustainable Development: The Role of Local Communities. UNESCO, 2017.

193. United Nations Educational, Scientific and Cultural Organization (UNESCO). (2003). Convention for the Safeguarding of the Intangible Cultural Heritage.

194. United Nations Development Programme (UNDP). (2008). Human Development Report 2007/2008: Fighting climate change: Human solidarity in a divided world

195. Constitution of Kenya 2010, Article 10

196. John Muthui & 19 others v County Government of Kitui & 7 others [2020] eKLR Para 129

197.Philippe Sands and Jacqueline Peel, Principles of International Environmental Law (4th Edition, CUP 2018) 197– 251.

198. Ibidem

199. Yann Kerbrat, Sandrine Maljean-Dubois. The Role of International Law in the Promotion of the Precautionary Principle. Carina Costa de Oliveira, Gabriela G. B. Lima Moraes, Fabrício Ramos Ferreira (dir.), A interpretação do princípio da precaução no direito brasileiro, no

direito comparado e no direito internacional, Pontes, pp. 275-284, 2019. ffhalshs-02342746f

200. Sadler, B. (1996). International Study of the Effectiveness of Environmental Assessment. Environmental Impact Assessment Review, 16(1), 5-21.

201. Glasson, J., Therivel, R., & Chadwick, A. (2012). Introduction to Environmental Impact Assessment. Routledge.

202. Millennium Ecosystem Assessment (MEA). (2005). Ecosystems and Human Well-being: Biodiversity Synthesis. World Resources Institute.

203. Intergovernmental Panel on Climate Change (IPCC). (2014). Climate Change 2014: Mitigation of Climate Change. Cambridge University Press.

204. John Muthui & 19 others v County Government of Kitui & 7 others [2020] eKLR Para 84.

205. Adrian Kamotho Njenga vs. Council of Governors & 3 others [2020] eKLR

206. Article 70 (1) of the Constitution of Kenya 2010

207. Article 70 (3) of the Constitution of Kenya 2010

208. Section 18 of the Environment and Land Court Act

209. Environmental Law by John Dleeson page 34

210. Section 93 of the Environmental Management and Co-Ordination Act.

211. The Environmental Management and Co-Ordination Act Chapter 387, Revised Edition 2012 [1999] Page E12 – 14.

212. Section 68 of The Environmental Management and Co-Ordination Act Chapter 387, Revised Edition 2012 [1999].

213. Section 68(2) of The Environmental Management and Coordination Act.

214. Section 68(3) of The Environmental Management and Coordination Act.
215. Section 68(4) of The Environmental Management and Coordination Act.
216. Section 69 of The Environmental Management and Coordination Act.
217. Adrian Kamotho Njenga vs. Council of Governors & 3 others [2020] eKLR Para 19
218. Constitution of Kenya (2010). Article 69. Nairobi: Government Printer.
219. Environmental Management and Coordination Act (EMCA) of 1999. Laws of Kenya, Cap. 387A. Nairobi: Government Printer.
220. Ogunkan, David V. "Achieving Sustainable Environmental Governance in Nigeria: A Review for Policy Consideration." Author Links Open Overlay Panel.
221. Narayan, D. (1995). The contribution of people's participation: Evidence from 121 rural water supply projects. Environmentally Sustainable Development Occasional Paper Series, No. 1. The World Bank.
222. United Nations Development Programme (UNDP). (2019). Human Development Report 2019: Beyond income, beyond averages, beyond today: Inequalities in human development in the 21st century.
223. Duflo, E. (2012). Women's empowerment and economic development. Journal of Economic Literature, 50(4), 1051-1079.
224. United Nations Development Programme (UNDP). (2019). Human Development Report 2019: Beyond income, beyond averages, beyond today: Inequalities in human development in the 21st century.
225. United Nations Educational, Scientific and Cultural Organization (UNESCO). (2006). Convention on the Diversity of Cultural Expressions.
226. World Bank. (2005). Indigenous Peoples, Poverty, and Human Development in Latin America: 1994-2004. World Bank

227. World Bank. (2015). The State of Social Safety Nets 2015. World Bank Group.

228. Sustainable Development in Kenya: Stocktaking in the run up to Rio+20

229. United Nations Framework Convention on Climate Change (UNFCCC). (2015). Paris Agreement. Retrieved from https://unfccc.int/process/the-paris-agreement/the-paris- agreement

230. U.S. Department of Energy. Energy Audits & Assessments. https://www.iea.org/ Reports/energy -efficiency-2021

231. Steady, Filomina Chioma, editor. Environmental Justice in the New Millennium: Global Perspectives on Race, Ethnicity, and Human Rights, page 4.

232. Ibidem

233. U.S. Department of Energy. "What is Environmental Justice?" Office of Legacy Management, U.S. Department of Energy, Retrieved from https://www.energy.gov/lm/what- environmental-justice#:~:text=Environmental%20justice%20is %20the%20fair,laws%2C%20regulations%2 C %20and%20policies.

234. Steady, Filomina Chioma, editor. Environmental Justice in the New Millennium: Global Perspectives on Race, Ethnicity, and Human Rights, page 9.

235. UNEP. "Environmental Rule of Law." http://www.unep.org/delc/worldcongress/ Home/ tabid/ 55710/ Default.aspx. Part II, 3rd

236. Bullard, Robert D. Dumping in Dixie: Race, Class, and Environmental Quality. Westview Press, 1990.

237. Johnson, Glenn S. Environmental Justice: A Brief History and Overview, page 17.

238. Mohai, Paul, David Pellow, and J. Timmons Roberts. "Environmental Justice." Annual Review of Environment and Resources, vol. 34, 2009, pp. 405-430.

239. Schlosberg, D. (2004). Reconceiving environmental justice: Global movements and political theories. Environmental Politics, 13(3), 517-540.

240. McDonald, David, editor. "Introduction." Environmental Justice in South Africa.

241. Ibidem

242. Ibidem

243. KM & 9 others v Attorney General & 7 others [2020] eKLR

244. Amnesty International. "Ogiek Case: Protection of an Indigenous Community in Kenya." Amnesty International, 2023, https://www.amnesty.org/en/latest/campaigns/2023/06/ogiek-case-protection-of-an-indigenous-community-in-kenya/#:~:text=After%20years%20of%20struggle%20with,cultural%20specificities%20must%20be%20protected.

245. Joseph Letuya & 21 others v Attorney General & 5 others [2014] eKLR

246. Joseph Leboo & 2 others v Director Kenya Forest Services & another

247. Martin Osano Rabera & Another vs. Municipal Council of Nakuru & 2 others [2018] eKLR

248. Constitution of Kenya, 2010, Article 42.

249. Constitution of Kenya, 2010, Article 22(1).

250. Constitution of Kenya, 2010, Article 42

251. Constitution of Kenya, 2010, Article 70(1).

252. Bullard, R. D. (1990). Dumping in Dixie: Race, Class, and Environmental Quality. Westview Press.

253. Schlosberg, D. (2004). Reconceiving Environmental Justice: Global Movements and Political Theories. Environmental Politics, 13(3), 517-540.

254. Mohai, P., Pellow, D., & Roberts, J. T. (2009). Environmental Justice. Annual Review of Environment and Resources, 34, 405-430.

255. Nanda, V., & Pring, G. (2013). International

Environmental Law and Policy for the 21st Century (2nd rev. ed.). Aspen Publishers.

256. United Nations. (1992). Rio Declaration on Environment and Development. United Nations Conference on Environment & Development.

257. Pring, G., & Pring, C. (2009). Greening Justice: Creating and Improving Environmental Courts and Tribunals (pp. 6-9). Retrieved from http://www.law.du.edu/ect-study.

258. United Nations Economic Commission for Europe (UNECE). (1998). Convention on Access to Information, Public Participation in Decision-Making and Access to Justice in Environmental Matters (Aarhus Convention). Retrieved from http://www.unece. org/env/pp/ documents /ce p 43e.pdf

259. Constitution of Kenya. (2010). Retrieved from http://www.kenyalaw.org:8181/exist/kenyalex/actview.xql?actid=Const2010.

260. Matters (Aarhus Convention). Retrieved from http://www.unece.org/env/pp/ documents/ cep43e.pdf.

261. Mohamed Ali Baadi and others v Attorney General & 11 Others [2018] eKLR

262. Ibid

263. Katiba Institute V Presidents Delivery Unit & 3 others [2017] eKLR

264. Sec 29 of the Environmental Management and Coordination Act. (1999). Retrieved from http://extwprlegs1.fao.org/docs/pdf/ken54647.pdf

265. Aarhus Convention on Access to Information, Public Participation in Decision-making and Access to Justice in Environmental Matters (1998).

266. Chega (Suing on their Own Behalf and as the Registered Official of Active Environment Team) v Kenya Forest Service & another; Kiambu Saw millers & 10 others (Interested Parties) (Constitutional Petition E053 of 2021) [2022] KEELC 13738 (KLR) (21 October 2022) (Judgment)

267. Constitution of Kenya (2010), Okiya Omtatah Okoiti v. Attorney General & 6 Others (2013) [2013] eKLR.

268. United Nations Environment Programme. (2019). Basel Convention on the Control of Transboundary Movements of Hazardous Wastes and Their Disposal.

269. United Nations. (1998). The Basel Convention on the Control of Transboundary Movements of Hazardous Wastes.

270. Pring, G. R., & Pring, C. (Year of publication). A Guide for Policy Makers. Global Environmental Outcomes LLC (GEO) and University of Denver Environmental Courts & Tribunals Study for the United Nations Environment Programme.

271. Article 162 (2) of The Constitution of Kenya 2010.

272. Article 162(2) (b) of the Constitution and Section 13 of the Environment and Land Court Act.

273. Article 162(2) (b) of the Constitution

274. Section 13(1) of the Environment and Land Court Act.

275. Section 13(2) of the Environment and Land Court Act.

276. Section 13 (3) of the Environment and Land Court Act.

277. Republic vs. Karisa Chengo & 2 Others [2017] eKLR

278. Section 13 of the Environment and Land Court Act (1)

279. Section 13(1) of The Environmental and Land Court Act.

280. National Land Commission v Afrison Export Import Limited& 10 others [2019] eKLR (para. 8)

281. Patricia Kameri-Mbote; 'the use of Criminal Law in Enforcing Environmental Law'; in Environmental Governance in Kenya, Implementing the Framework Law, ed. C.O. Okidi, et al.

282. Professors George (Rock) Pring & Catherine (Kitty) Pring, University of Denver Environmental Courts and Tribunal Study and Global Environmental

Outcomes LLC. UN Environment guide to Specialized Environmental Courts and Tribunals

283. Section 125 of the Environment Management and Coordination Act of 1999.

284. Justice Antonio Herman Benjamin, High Court of Brazil, available online at http://digitalcommons.pace.edu/pelr/vol29/iss2/8 at 584.

285. Section 125(1) of The Environmental Management and Coordination Act of 1999

286. Article 42 of The Constitution of Kenya 2010

287. Section 13(3) of the Environmental and Land Court Act.

288. Environmental Law and Policy" by James Salzman and Barton H. Thompson Jr.

289. Environmental Regulation: Law, Science, and Policy" by Robert V. Percival, Christopher

H. Schroeder, Alan S. Miller, and James P. Leape.

290. Ryland's Vs Fletcher (1861-73) ALL ER REPI is the Locus on the Principle of Strict Liability. Any person who keeps anything in unnatural circumstances has to bear the full consequences of the liability that arises if the things that he keeps escapes to his neighbor's land and causes injury.

291. The court has affirmed the principle of strict liability as relates to the law in Redlands vs. Fletcher in KM & 9 others v Attorney General & 7 Others [2020] eKLR.

292. MC Mehta Vs Union of India (1987) 1 SCC 395.

293. The Supreme Court of India has emphasized the concept of Absolute liability in the case of MC Mehta Vs Union of India (1987) 1 SCC 395.

294. Constitution of Kenya 2010, Article 22(1)

295. Constitution of Kenya 2010, Article 22 (3)

296. The Land and Environment Act, Section 13(7)

297. Sands, Philippe, and Pierre Klein. "Bowett's Law of International Institutions." (2009).

298. Brown Weiss, Edith. "In Fairness to Future Generations: International Law, Common Patrimony, and Intergenerational Equity." (1989).

299. Sand, Peter H., and Marc B. Maresca. "The Precautionary Principle and International Law: The Challenge of Implementation." (2002).

300. Boyle, Alan E., and Michael R. Anderson. "Human Rights Approaches to Environmental Protection." (2008).

301. Epps, Tracey. "Environmental Compliance in International Law: Lessons from the WTO." (2006).

302.

303. Section 118 of the public Health Act

304. Section 118 (e) Ibid

305. Section 118 (h) Ibid

306. Section 119 Ibid

307. Section 120 (1) Ibid

308. Section 120(3) Ibid

309. United Nations. (2015). Transforming our World: The 2030 Agenda for Sustainable Development. Resolution adopted by the General Assembly on 25 September 2015. A/RES/70/1.

310. United Nations. (2015). Transforming our World: The 2030 Agenda for Sustainable Development. Resolution adopted by the General Assembly on 25 September 2015. A/RES/70/1.

311. Ibidem

312. Ibidem

313. Ibidem

314. Ibidem

315. Ibidem